Selected Poems

FIONA PITT-KETHLEY was born in 1954. She studied at the Chelsea School of Art where she obtained a BA (hons) before going on to become a full-time writer. As a student she ushered at the Old Vic and National Theatre. While writing, she sometimes worked as a film extra. She married the chess grandmaster and former British chess champion, James Plaskett, in 1995. They have a son, Alexander. In 2002 they moved to Spain. At first they lived in an ex-pat area until driven out by tyre-slashing English and Irish pensioners. They are now much happier living amongst the Spanish in Cartagena where they have adopted seven feral cats.

Since moving to Spain, Fiona has acquired new hobbies: she practices Kyokushin karate and goes rock-hunting and hill-walking in the Sierra Minera, an area she is currently writing a book on. She also enjoys fishing for her dinner, listening to local Flamenco concerts and snorkels for several months of the year.

Also by Fiona Pitt-Kethley

SELECTED POETRY COLLECTIONS
Sky Ray Lolly (1986)
Private Parts (1987)
The Perfect Man (1989)
Dogs (1993)
Double Act (1996)
Memo From a Muse (1997)

NOVELS
The Misfortunes of Nigel (1991)
Baker's Dozen (2000)

TRAVEL WRITING
Journeys to the Underworld (1988)
The Pan Principle (1994)
Red Light Districts of the World (2000)

COLLECTED JOURNALISM
Too Hot to Handle (1992)

AUTOBIOGRAPHY
The Autobiography of Fiona Pitt-Kethley : My Schooling (2000)

ANTHOLOGIES (AS EDITOR)
Literary Companion to Sex : An Anthology of Prose and Poetry (1992)
Literary Companion to Low Life (1995)

Selected Poems

FIONA PITT-KETHLEY

SALT

CAMBRIDGE

PUBLISHED BY SALT PUBLISHING
PO Box 937, Great Wilbraham, Cambridge CB21 5JX United Kingdom

© Fiona Pitt-Kethley, 2008

The right of Fiona Pitt-Kethley to be identified as the
author of this work has been asserted by her in accordance
with Section 77 of the Copyright, Designs and Patents Act 1988.

First published 2008

Printed and bound in the United Kingdom by Biddles Ltd, Kings Lynn, Norfolk

Typeset in Swift 9.5 / 13

ISBN 978 1 84471 453 7 hardback

Salt Publishing Ltd gratefully acknowledges
the financial assistance of Arts Council England

1 3 5 7 9 8 6 4 2

For James and Alexander

Contents

Acknowledgements

Many of these poems were published previously in *Sky Ray Lolly* (1986), *Private Parts* (1987), *The Perfect Man* (1989), *Dogs* (1993), *Double Act* (1996) and *Memo From a Muse* (1997). Many also appeared in magazines such as *Literary Review*, *The London Review of Books*, *New Statesman*, *Spare Rib* and *The Spectator*.

Sky Ray Lolly

A toddler on a day out in Herne Bay,
on seeing an ancient, civil-servant-type,
I held my Sky Ray lolly—red, yellow
and green striped, pointed, dripping down between
my legs and walked bandy. My Ma and Pa
(old-fashioned innocents like Rupert Bear's)
just didn't notice this and ambled on,
that is, until they saw the old man's face,
jaw dislocated in surprise. They grabbed
that Martian's willy from my little hand.

The world still sees me as a nasty kid
usurping maleness. A foul brat to be
smacked down by figures of authority.
All things most natural in men, in me
are vice—having no urge to cook or clean,
lacking maternal instincts.

And they would take my pride, my rocket
of ambition, amputate my fun and geld
my laughter, depriving me of colour.
And smirk to see my little lolly melt,
me left with a stick.

[1]

Baby Doll

My cousin sent a baby doll for me —
hairless and clammy, waxen yellowish-grey
with sunken pale blue eyes and a mouth pursed
for pouring water in so it came out
through a small aperture between its legs.

I called it Peter, though it had no prick.
It looked too ugly for a girl, I thought.
I used to fill it up and souse my lap.
Sometimes I'd press its squashy latex head
to force the liquid out at higher speed,
yellowing the pee by adding mustard in,
or making diarrhoea with chocolate milk.
Sometimes it vomited and pissed at once.

At last, my mother took my toy away,
afraid I'd show it to some visitor.
Several days later, it was back again,
seated amongst my other dolls and bears.
She'd used half an old shoe dye on his face,
giving him hair and beard, and togged him out
with a sharp suit of black and white checked tweed.
'Peter's grown up,' she said.
'Adults don't wet themselves.'

His lips looked red against his blue-black beard.
You can do anything at any age, I thought.
I filled him up again. He peed,
marking his breeches with a yellow stain.

Pigeons

I used to love to watch their delicate
shades of grey as they swaggered on the lawn,
jostling for bits of bread I'd left for them.
I'd lean on the chipped chocolate brown sill
and name them to myself as Arthur's knights—
the same set came there every day—Gawain,
Lancelot, Perceval and Galahad,
a white one—Guinevere.

I made my parents tell me bird stories—
'Belinda the demon pigeon of Acton
lived above a gargoyle in a graveyard . . .'
reassured by repetition before
reading widened my choice. I searched upstairs,
(my father used to coo realistically
and thought of bringing a clay pigeon home
to plant on the mahogany wardrobes,
just peeping down, but out of reach.) One day,
in the way that stories sometimes come true,
a grounded pigeon hobbled through the door.
We kept her in a box in a back room.
Close up, I decided, birds weren't so nice.
She pecked our hands for food and glared at us
with her red eyes. I never liked her much.
The room began to smell of feathers and shit.
She took a lover too—a ponce of a pigeon—
we nicknamed him Albert, I don't know why.
He would puff out his petrol-shaded chest,
come in through the open window, rape her,
knock her about a bit, then steal her seed.
That was if the cat didn't tumble her first.

The vet just broke her neck. 'The best way,' he said,
standing there, the limp bird in his hands.
'She wouldn't have flown again.' My father
came home angry, buried her box and all,
calling him a wretched amateur.

If I pass the dirty-grey wallowing mass
in Trafalgar Square and hear the rattle
of seed in tins I remember Lucy
and feel disgust, some fear perhaps—not quite
a phobia—disgust at her cold end
before my father's eyes, fear at her role
of victim, a lot which could be anyone's.

Thoughts After a Burglary
For my father

In a recent break-in, some tapes of mine
were stolen, one of which contained the last
and only record of my father's voice.

He took me as a child to the sights
of London, obvious and minor, churches
of every sect, strange shops and restaurants,
tutoring me in feats of endurance —
eating the hottest Madras curries
at a tender age, swallowing a quart of pop
without taking my mouth off the bottle,
bagpipe impersonations in subways,
writing things on graffiti-proof tiling,
tearing tin cans in half and lobbing them
into the passing goods trains, and so on.

The memories are all blurred now, but there's
just enough to leave me with a strange sense
of déjà vu in any part of London.

There were once yearly parties too,
where he'd clown as Charlie Chaplin before
the little beasts from my snob school — walking
in suddenly, tripping over a raped
and ruptured, Egyptian leather pouffé
(with pictures of camels and pyramids
and people all turned sideways for the tourists)
he'd somersault, all sixteen stone of him,
the laughter of the kids enough payment
as they sat, venomous in nylon frills.

In time, he lost his journalist's job. He'd
lived in the shadow of his successful
father — self-made, writer of ripping yarns,
fifty years editor of *The Wide World.*

And we got poorer in a time when dole
was not the norm. Later—a short term job—
educational précis, took him to
London's technical libraries. I went
with him in the holidays, quietly
reading odd manuals, dictionaries,
whatever was available, staring
in a trance at Adam ceilings, or out
through high windows at warehouses with doors
opening, four storeys up, on to nothing.

Then followed years, a phrenetic period of
letter-writing for jobs, the sending of
curricula vitae, getting up at
dawn, endless endless letters, and at night,
putting a slop-pail of vast and bloody lights
(bought for our cats dirt-cheap from a friendly
butcher who enjoyed Dad's filthy jokes)
against the back-door to stop the burglars.

My father, a pensioner, at last, turned
cat-herd with some twelve furry apostles.
My parents moved out of London then,
while I was away at Art School. The thieves
my father dreaded hit in the new place—
not clean like London ones—these scattered papers,
tore and destroyed, dumped books out in the rain.
They took almost every little thing he owned:
his bits and bobs of militaria,
all the pomposity of the Army
vanishing into a thief's pocket.

After a slow and gradual depression,
a month before my twenty-first birthday,
his heart gave out. Sensing something
I had come home a day early. We found him
lying on the lavatory floor, a livid cut
where he had struck his face in falling,
in shirt and pullover a size too small.
The undertaker took him in a pushchair
like a baby.

Some cats outlasted him and I became
their gravedigger—a new role thrust on me.
The last, a lame, alcoholic she-cat
who'd lacerated his back into
a Grünewald Crucifixion, lingered for years,
and ran to meet me every time I sang
in imitation of my father's voice.

The thieves contributed to rob me
of my ally, silencing him twice over.
What's left? A strong enduring influence—
a part of my voice that's his.

The Fox

My father took a walk one autumn day
In leafy woods in Bucks, down Amersham way.
And while he answered Nature's Call, he saw
A limping vixen with a wounded paw.
She crossed a muddy stream and went to earth
Down in the den where she had given birth.
Her cubs were there, crying and cowering in fear—
They heard the baying of the hounds draw near.
And as my father stood and buttoned his fly,
The Master of the Hunt came coursing by.
He reined his mare in by my father's side:
'Seen 'im?' he yelled. 'Seen who?' my Dad replied.
'The fox, you fool!' he stormed (not being local,
He'd taken my father for some dim-wit yokel).
A truthful bloke, for once, Dad lied like Nixon,
And sent him to the right to save the vixen.
And soon there followed on a motley crew
On borrowed nags, all shouting: 'View Halloo!'—
Yuppy developers, hoping to look posh,
No breeding, balls or brains, just loads of dosh.
      Foxes, are rascals, stealing where they can,
      But, on the whole, they do less harm than Man.

The Mask

After my grandpa's death, my father found
a Chinese cardboard mask and copy
of Krafft-Ebbing locked in Newnes's office safe.

Respectably alcoholic, 'Old Vic'
read his 'review copies' though *The Wide World*
never did reviews, drank champagne solo
and indulged in japes of an Edwardian
character—painting extra figures
in a convincing style on Christmas cards
to freak the guests. Not content with editing,
he'd talk of writing other books. (His first,
written under other names—The Captain,
Sidney York, Rupert Chesterton
and Singleton Carew—were ripping yarns
where villains smuggled saccharin, or tales
of lands where the heroes always cried
'Caramba!', Incas or derring-do at sea.)

Twice weekly he would take the train to work,
passing his friend, a retired editor,
rearing rhubarb at Rickmansworth with young
and pretty 'Nursie' at his side (his heart
was bad). As the train slowed Vic would rise, wave
in some new disguise, his George-Burns-face screwed
up as Nelson, a penny at one eye,
arm in a sling and a paper cocked hat.
Then he'd put the lot away and sit back.
Tailored and toupéed—he was the perfect
image of the City gent, till sickness
took him on that journey where there are
no masks—no Fu Manchu or Charlie Chan
to hide behind.

The Ecumenical Movement

My first years were haunted by foreign names,
phrases like 'apostolical succession'
and strange invasions of dressed-up prelates.
After a quick ordination, blessing
or what have you in the chapel, they'd go
out the back to take their photographs.
(I liked the geometry or our garden—
first, the square washing-line that wouldn't spin,
then the two apple trees set in the lawn
forming a triangle with the pear outside
the circle of a fairy ring.) They'd stand
there more or less, say 'cheese' in their mitres,
copes and glasses, then troop inside for tea.

I was usually bored so I'd put on
a kind of cabaret—lick out the jam
from tarts, striptease, bring in a brimming pot,
sexually harass the better-looking men
except when some Ukrainian Count was due
and I was sent to Margate with my Mum.

My father's hobby was the marrying
of sect to sect, patching up old schisms
to make a whole and undivided church.
(He even asked Ian Paisley to join
in a wonderful stroke of naivety
or taking the piss—(I've never quite known which.)

He held vast correspondences with priests,
archbishops, curés and archimandrites,
all of the smallest denominations.

The American ones gave him degrees,
the Russians, magazines he couldn't read,

the Italians, titles. Duc de Deauville
was the prettiest.

Our chapel was in the slope of the roof
with tatty repro-icons spaced around,
a pale oak-veneered altar touched by worm,
bottled holy water, rose oil chrysm
and souvenir crosses on the mantelpiece
above a small gas fire, and a huge loop
of light-cord trailing from a naked bulb.

My mother rarely liked my father's friends.
One of them brought his 'favourite choirboy'
to see the London sights. 'We always sleep
in separate beds,' he said defensively.
He sat there with his leg wagging
and left a little damp spot on the chair.
(We kept that seat solely for visitors
like a Siege Perilous. Eventually
we sold the dining-room set to knockers.)
Another, a most frequent visitor,
we heard had got married to a black girl
and was ashamed of her and kept her down
the basement of his Fulham house — her
and their two children. To his friends he was still
a hapless bachelor scrounging free meals.
(I spoilt that though by forging Christmas cards
to all those friends from him 'and family'.)
The last I heard he was selling hair oil
through ads on the back of a literary mag.
One man decided to christen my Dad
Mar Rupertus — 'Mar' he said, was Persian
for Lord. (He called his cat Mar Pluto too.)

I always liked my father's weird parcels—
strange stamps and seals and semi-papal bulls,
the family trees of those descended from
Avignon popes (all covered in gold-leaf),
an altar-cloth depicting all Christ's wounds
to be embroidered in red silken thread—

a sort of kit that came with a small bone
from St Eutychius. I have it still.
I hardly like to throw the thing away.
(How hard to deal with the small useless bits
that people leave behind them when they go!
I have a superstition about waste
so bunged a contraceptive pack and odd
cigars in handbags at some jumble sale
to give their purchasers a nice surprise.)

Sometimes it was like living on the edge
of a thriller. One Frenchman wrote about
his long campaign to convert Lucifer
and told us he was getting near his aim.
Next thing we read he'd been knocked down and killed
upon some Paris street. And Mum received
a shaky note from nice old Doctor Crowe—
it must have been the last he wrote—saying
he'd give me 'lessons in magic'.

And there was the 'autonic eye' we kept
stashed in the coal cellar for years. Seemed much
the size and shape of a well-wrapped severed head,
I thought. (I used to read a lot of Poe.)
A bishop from South Africa had asked
if we would mind the thing, bribing us first
with a big box of grapes and a large tin
of chocolate fingers.

Bums

My Head, Miss Harold, five foot square in grey,
was deeply disappointed that the shrink
she had me sent to certified me sane.
(At seven, I'd written 'BUM' upon my desk,
and that, in Old Harry's view meant madness.)
'They pluck these words' she said, 'out of the air!'
(That was the only time she didn't use
'If however . . .' her Johnsonian catchphrase.)
'Perhaps,' my mother said, 'she got it from
A Midsummer Night's Dream?' The Head just blinked.
What had she missed? The school editions were
all bowdlerised. My mother was quite wrong.
I'd only read Hamlet—no comedies—
and that play does not, as I remember,
have a bum, or even the ghost of one.
Like any normal child, I'd plucked, (Miss H.
was right), that word out of the air while I
was playing Bums—a game where little girls
(or boys) compare size, shape and texture bared.
Ma should have known—she once caught three of us,
standing, minus our navy knickers
in a front-room window, near the piano.
(I don't remember if we planned to play.)
Startled we saw a white face staring in
between the pink hydrangeas and the road.

Evolution

'Some men are very wicked!' my Gran said
while looking at a monkey in the zoo.
His spectacles of flesh and blue behind
reminded her of someone she once knew.

Apples

Where are the old apples,
the conical, uneven apples, obscurely ribbed,
ripening to deeper yellow, the crimson-cheeked apples,
marbled and washed with clear red,
the deep lively green apples,
strewed with silvery scales,
dark-spotted, speckled like hens,
brownish, orange-tinged against the sun,
veined in grey russet, angular, smooth-skinned,
the transparent apples grown on sand,
the Bantam's-egg-sized apples,
the child's-head-sized apples,
the red-fleshed Sops-in-Wine,
anise-flavoured New Rock Pippin,
fennel Ross Nonpareil,
Pitmaston Pine Apple, balsamic Sack and Sugar,
the strawberry and violet flavoured Calville apples,
the waxen-yellow aromatic Gravenstein,
transparent as porcelain,
pine-flavoured Lord Burghley, musky Reinette Franche,
homely Costard, Catshead, Hoary Morning,
Nanny, Cockpit, Hall Door, Bedfordshire Foundling?

On the shelves are our apples—the apples we deserve,
thin-stalked, unctuous, even green, polished to an inconsistency,
flesh sub-acid, cardboard-pipped, eyes stamenless,
sweating under the lights like a crowd of nervous actors.

Giant Hogweed

My teacher, wholemeal-faced and nature-crazed
brought wings into our fish-tank classroom just
to show their workings — she'd no sense of smell.
A friend had sent them her by parcel post:
a pigeon's, sparrows' and a kingfisher's.
(It seemed all wrong that halcyon feathers
should stink just as much as any city bird's.)

I tried to look for things to brighten up
the school and put my weekend's fungi in
our bath. (I thought to keep them fresh.)
Broad Dryad's Saddle, Cep with its bun top,
the mealy-warted Blusher bruising pink,
a Shaggy Ink-Cap like a lawyer's wig,
Tawny Grisettes and Beef-Steak Fungus from
an oak, all turned to slime by Monday's light.

Later, a Giant Hogweed caught my eye —
at eight, I loathed the catkins good kids brought.
Miss Davies, too never believed my tales:
the bullfinch was a chaffinch on my tree,
the raven but a carrion crow. As for
the carpet-wetting wallaby I saw
at Christmas in the Lyric Theatre —
'Well, really!'

My sci-fi weed had a cool reception.
I'd lugged it on the 207 bus,
its seven-foot stalk trailing across the seats,
my father held the end, I had the flower.)
A show-off's bloom, too tall, too poisonous,
no fit companion for the sensible
contents of the nature table. They stood
it in the corner by itself.

A Sunday Afternoon

Seeking adventures one church-free Sunday,
I crossed the Dives-Lazarus divide
from Ealing into Acton on the bike
I had for winning a free place at ten,
and chained it up to Springfield Gardens' gate.
It was your average London park, complete
with flasher, park-keeper, geraniums,
a bum-splintering see-saw and baby swings.
I soon got talking, and a girl of seven
was pointed out, who always dressed in pink
and used to suck men's willies in the Gents.
I thought it seemed a funny thing to do.

The boys didn't use the swings or see-saw,
but stood a little way off, watching us,
hands in pockets. An Indian twelve-year-old
crossed the gulf sniggering and asked
if he could 'plant his carrot in my turnip field'.

Soon, we were rescued from moral danger;
the 'Firebrands' evangelists descended
asking the question 'Are you saved?' We weren't
too sure, and so they kidnapped and bussed us
to Acton's Co-op Hall for Sunday School.
A gaggle of children, matted or plaited,
our hands reeking of the metal swing-chains,
we were ready to try anything once
and sang 'I will make you fishers of men',
even the little cocksucker in pink.

Taking Off

Sometimes, spontaneously, a group of girls
gathered in the playground. Half a dozen
or more pairs stood, grasping each others' wrists.
No-one ever really suggested it
and we never knew the name of the game.

When your turn came round you'd take off and dive,
landing on a mattress of arms to be
tossed several times before their holds slackened
and you slid down twisting on to the grass.
With your eyes shut you felt you were flying.
I could never understand why Tom Brown
didn't enjoy being tossed in a blanket,
except, tastes differ.

That game was considered too physical.
Like leapfrog and friendships with older girls
the teachers always put a stop to it.

The Staff Room had a squarish bay-window
which looked out on the grass where we played.
Daily one hot summer, two girls lay there
in each others' arms, kissing, mouths open,
a button or two of their turquoise blouses
left casually undone, their hands straying
occasionally inside—blatant—you'd think
they'd have saved it for some empty classroom
separating quickly if a prefect
came through the door.

The grass they always lay on parched yellow.
Daily we waited for the skies to fall.
The Head would delegate the job, we thought,
and send a minion to prise them apart.

There were various legends extant about
people who'd been expelled for cannabis,
abortions and calling the English teacher
a cow, (brave on a quart of Woodpecker).
That pair obviously just had it coming.

One day, after Prayers, as we sat cross-legged
on the parquet listening to notices,
in a roundabout sort of way the Head
gave out she'd seen something that might upset
the people in a block of flats nearby
and give a wrong impression of the school.
We pricked up our ears. 'Some of you,' she said,
'have been taking off your white ankle socks
in public, on the grass.'

Ghost Train

I flirted with horror on ghost trains,
relishing the caresses of cobwebs,
laughing through electronic screams.

How individual each man's view of fear—
the plastic skeletons at every turn,
lions painted on double swinging doors,
(once even, a plastic girl in bra and pants,
a skull beneath her wig when she swung round).

The catharsis of terror is over
so quickly—not spun out like life. You come
to light from darkness, walk even ground
after the Crazy House's corridors
and tilted spongy floors.

Red Fish

At thirteen I bought a tuppenny packet
containing two red fish with instructions
from an old shabby newsagent's in Cork,
where they sold copies of *The Red Letter*
(romantic nurse and doctor stories
with Orphan Annie on the back), odd eggs,
bacon, (priced by the rasher not the pound)
and ice-white Chilly Willy lollies.

The cellophane fish curled in my hot palms:
the pack declared me 'Passionate'. Next term,
I took them into school. We used to try
sex quizzes out of mags. (You either lied
or were humiliated by lowish scores.
The ones who'd brought them in, mysteriously,
would come out tops.) My two red fish labelled
my friends 'Indifferent', 'Cold' or even 'Dead'.

At that stage, most of us tried no *real* tests.
Made cruel by religion I'd indulge
in the longest kisses and little else,
stopping myself the only way I could,
turning to rigor mortis in boys' arms—
too gauche even to say the reason why,
cold as the fish in other people's hands.

Life's harder when your body's reflexes
become the points of proof, with men
who dutifully ask you if you've come
(why can't they tell?)—and then dispute your 'Yes'
because they think your chest's not flushed enough,
or pride themselves your nipples are erect,
forgetting that they'd left the heating off.

Swimming Baths

In Acton, the Public Baths' attendant
was not the life-guard type you might expect.
You'd see his fishy, chlorinated eyes
above the doors. He'd got it to an art
parading past the cubicles, checking
the locks still worked, peering at ground level
for extra pairs of feet.

A serious few entered with a low dive,
thrusting forward, their heads in wrinkled caps,
their bodies smeared with Vaseline. The rest
were there to touch. Strangers, shrunken in trunks,
would push you in, splash you, hold you under
until you nearly drowned—just wholesome fun.
Swimmers, whose only small talk's sadists' tales
of cocks sucked down the deep end's outlet hole,
(their owners had the choice—lose it or drown)
and razors stuck in water-chutes that carved
girl divers neatly into halves and filled
the pool with blood, staining it for all time,
you'd see them leaving, gripping damp towels,
red-rimmed as syphilitics from the Baths'
cocktail of pee.

My school's pool was politer. We had to
empty our bladders first, (whether we could
or not), and march through anti-verruca stuff.
On Open Days the fathers could be seen
training expensive cine cameras
on older girls emerging from the water,
wet straggles of pubic hair across their thighs,
missing the moment when their scrawnier kids
came first in Crawl. Our aquamarine swim-suits,

(the Head's design) old-fashioned but not decent,
had hooks and straps which slipped when water-logged,
or came undone one side, leaving a breast exposed.

Charity

Our school was very hot on charity,
its Scripture Room was always stuffed with knits
and poison-lilac bath-salts screwed in jars.
(My Alma Mater had adopted some
Korean orphans and each autumn term
held the 'Korean Sale' in aid of them.
Their mission sent a photo every year;
they all had specs and western-Christian frocks.
The ambassador's daughter once came too,
to thank us all on their behalf. She was
the only other Korean we had seen
and looked a little different in chic silk.)

At eight, we made small candleholders out
of clay. Our teacher took us to a hut
beside the emptied swimming bath, where the
caretaker used to hang his uprooted
tomato plants to ripen in the showers.
(His small green fruit never seemed to make it
past yellow.) Our fingers bleached and crinkled
rolling grey balls on boards muddied with slip.
We who were only used to the homely
hot-cats'-piles aroma of plasticine
smelt mortality lodged under our nails.

The years passed in weekly donations, sales
and Harvest Festivals of windfalls for
the hospitals, bonked tins for Acton's Old.
And 'Dorcas' when we made tiny garments
with large needles and larger hands. Each form
did a lurid layette for the Third World—
a lemon Orlon matinée jacket,
pink shawl, blue dress and Bri-Nylon bootees . . .

I went along with it until the Sixth,
when greater action was required. Most thought
I was a shit for opting out, but yet,
I couldn't take the thought of forcibly
redecorating flats in my own choice
of colour scheme for frightened OAPs,
or giving Christmas gifts in Old Folks' homes
of pencils taped to soap made by The Blind.

Tragedy

My father, a Philistine journalist,
(as his father and grandfather were before),
took me to see *Romeo and Juliet*.
'What a shame about that nice young couple,'
he said. 'Why *did* they have to die!'

Tragedy's quite addictive in its way:
the irritation keeps you reading on.
I went through Hardy at an early age
hoping to find one book at least where things
weren't buggered up for all the characters.
Heroes and heroines are not ill-starred—
they're just dishonest, never talk things out—
that's all.

'But don't you realise,' I told my Dad,
(I was a cynical fourteen), 'that pair'd have bred.
There'd be a million fools by now,
all horribly romantic as the first,
all trying to spoil their own or others' lives.'

'I think they should have changed the end' he said,
'for modern audiences.'

Dirty Old Men

Old men, the dirty kind, come in two sorts—
the nice ones and the nasty. They're much like
those who pass by a fruit stall. Some just think
how nice an apple would have been if they'd
had teeth. Others without the wherewithal
to buy or eat, must sink their grimy thumbs
into the nectarines.

On Charing Cross an English wino said:
'You've got charisma . . . just like me.' Elsewhere,
a Polish drunk, stretched happy on a bench,
called me 'A real lady' when I passed
him back the cherry wine he'd dropped. I'd say
these were both nice ones of the dirty type.
Likewise an English master I once knew.
I was to play Titania at his school.
He wished to have the fairies in the show
all starkers, me too, and painted silver.
The governors refused, he settled for
transparent lamé catsuits, Mary Quant.
I had a most uncomfortable time—
Cobweb and Co made me a fakir's bed
with pins. (The sight of me, laddered into
indecency, getting a leg over
poor Bottom made the local vicar blanch—
I was a leading light in his church choir.)

This teacher had a wall at home, filled up
with codpieces he'd made—just for the play.
And most were much too big, for Puck kept all
his Strepsils down his and we heard them roll
with every cartwheel and each somersault.

The other sort—made asses by their own
illusions in the winter of their years,
not hooked on Shakespeare or the bottle's joys,
are not content with dreams, must pry and poke,
place their corpse-withered lips upon your cheek,
their grave-claws on your shoulders. Like old goats,
they chumble and spoil everything they touch,
blaming some Circe for their beastliness.

'The Hidden Persuaders'

I was one of the Oxbridge stream at school.
We were taken off for extra classes,
mainly to groom us for The Interview
and general essays we might have to write.

First, they checked we took the right newspapers
(*Times*, *Guardian*, *Daily Telegraph*)
not ones with pieces on randy vicars.
Then, we were handed out a list of books,
all modern, serious but popular,
those that could tell us what we ought to think,
things like Vance Packard's *The Hidden Persuaders*,
The Female Eunuch and *The Naked Ape*.
(I still avoid the titles on that list.)
I buggered off, read Jacobean plays:
Beaumont and Fletcher were much more my taste.

I was reminded of a magazine:
'Anne wants to smarten up for her new job'.
Dog's-dinnered generally and blushered-up,
shes stuffed into a yellow suit and heels;
her hair is layered like feathers and highlighted.
Anne says that she is 'pleased with her new look'.
She would—to get away.

We were all studying for A-levels—
three each at least. In my case it was four—
Latin and Greek, Religious Knowledge, Art.
'Art doesn't count,' they said. 'Why don't you give it up?'
(Better to be some wanker with a First
from Cambridge than a Michelangelo?)
I gave the lot up and went in for Art.
I'll wash my own brains, thank you very much.

Private Parts

Pencil is less ambiguous than paint,
incising hard lines round the genitals.
I've seen art students, broad-minded enough
to talk naturally to naked models
in their breaks from posing, become furtive
as they draw a penis—men too. Often,
like children cheating in exams, one hand
shielded the other's workings from all view.
Others erased madly—they'd made it far
too short or long, then found they'd worked
the paper to a grubby thinness there,
or left black rubber pills like pubic lice.

Marble's cold and doesn't change however hard
you stare at it—an easier task than flesh
to draw. Sketching a Roman Mercury
in the Fitzwilliam, I'd toyed with the thighs
for far too long, eyed by some soldier
from a US base nearby. He stood until
I gravitated to the balls, then pounced.
An ugly human, he'd identified
with the smooth body of a god, the image
on the paper, seeing my pencil's touch
as a caress.

Beards

I have doubts about kissing men with beards.
It seems like cunnilingus when their lips protrude
from mousy hair.

Most women have brown pubics, even blondes.
I know this from my four years at Art School.
Once though, we had a model whose hair was
the brightest shade of red against white skin.

The teacher, with his curly, mousy beard—
more like the real thing than hers—arranged
her propped on one hip in a cold-sheeted,
blue-white bed, tipped up like a fishmonger's
marble slab, chalking her pose on the cloth.

Through the weeks that followed, we saw her bruise
like a plum through the weight of her body.
And the brown-bearded teacher asked me why
I was more interested in structure than
the sensual texture of her skin.

The Face Below

While drawing nudes in Art School I could see
A second face on each stare back at me,
With navel nostrils, twinkling nipple eyes,
A grinning crease where torso meets the thighs.
Some looked quite glum, while others gave a smile;
Males stuck their tongues out with expressions vile.
Often, a model on a Windsor chair
Wearing a string of pearls and well-coiffed hair,
Looked too demure a type of woman to know
The bearded lady smirking down below.

A Piece of Jade

The first class in a course on Chinese Art—
we sat around, fulsomely holding forth
on tiny objects that our tutor'd brought,
all small enough to be hand held by us,
useful things, he'd said, everyday objects,
some obvious, some not, all well-crafted,
carved and polished to great smoothness.
One struck us by its simple elegance;
our Philippino lecturer looked on,
amused by our pretentiousness. (Although,
we later heard the tale of how he'd won
a grant to set up an illicit still
and urinated at a festival,
distilled it, drunk it and then peed again—
a symbol of the earth's renewal, of course—
and, if you're not too squeamish, a nice way
to earn your bread.) He soon let out, the long
and subtly-polished piece of jade I held
was an old arsehole-stopper from a corpse,
set there to keep the evil spirits out.

Cherry Trees

The specious charm of cherry trees with their
drain-clogging, Andrex-coloured blossoming
leaves me unmoved. I can't say that I blame
George Washington, or, my father who
nobbled our London one by pruning it.
The week-long shower drives me up ladders
to shift the putrid, pink confetti-gunge
that stops the gutters up. Although I take
a saw to our St Leonards one, break down
branches and make spitting fires from them,
the thing just grows and burgeons horribly,
poking its voyeuristic tips against
our neighbour's place. They're easy-going, but . . .
I was quite glad when Polly, next-door's cat,
(a ginger-mutant-she from Dungeness),
ran up and piddled through our bannisters
from three floors up, down on my fresh-washed hair—
it gave me something every bit as bad
as that foul tree, for a complaint if I
should need one—there were witnesses.

I wish I had just half the strength of those
who handled scenery at the Old Vic.
Superbly philistine, they saw each play
in terms of overtime, and Chekhov as
'A load of bloody cherry trees to shift!'

French Connection

On our way to see *French Connection II*,
a friend of mine stopped off in Leicester Square
and bought a large vibrator from a shop.
The three of us went in together.
We stood by while the assistant talked
and talked of the advantages of a massage,
and managed in ten minutes not to say
anything dirty — all euphemisms.
Eventually she sold my friend a kind
much larger, dearer and with varied heads,
not only that, but also a long sheath —
bubucled latex, black as liquorice,
warty enough to be the Elephant Man's.
'It's realistic and reduced,' she said.
She put that mandrake in a box full of
neat polystyrene grooves for other bits,
and packaged it in paper — candy-striped.
The cinema was round the corner and
as usual then, the usher searched our bags,
(those were the IRA bomb days). Seeing
the innocent, shoe-box-shaped package there,
he laughed and let it by untouched.

La Vie Bohème

Some arty type had said he wished to buy
a large Expressionistic nude I'd done,
but changed his bloody mind. So I was stuck.
Carrying canvasses is quite an art—
I held its stretcher by the middle bar,
hoping the wind wouldn't catch it like a sail.

I was pissed off enough to take a drink
off Dracula so I propped up my daub
against a café wall in the King's Road
when an old artist offered me coffee.
He gave his name and then declared with pride,
'Modigliani painted my arsehole once!'
'How come?' I said. 'Like this—when I was young
my famous uncle who adopted me
was friends with him, let him mind me one day.
He took me to the Paris Zoo. I saw
the new white rhino there and shat my pants
with fear. He brought me to his studio
and cleaned me up with a large whitewash brush.
That's how!'

He drew my portrait next—I have it still—
my face (or anyone's) surrounded by
a moon, a star, a cow, a fiddle and a fish,
all done in lilac fibre-tip,
'avec toute mon affection' scrawled beside.

Then he proposed that I should marry him,
hinting that he had plenty in the bank.
'You could just pose for me,' he said. 'I'm much
too old to do a thing. You could just lie
or stand there while I read you Robert Burns.'

Cockroaches

The Stalls crowd eating salmon at the bar
suspected nothing of the teeming mass,
a cast of thousands underneath the fridge
that held their ices for the interval,
their chocolate, strawberry and vanilla tubs.
One night, some careless usher dropped his change;
we had to move the thing to get it up.
Out came the cockroaches, big, little, large,
by ones and twos at first, dazed by the lights,
they straggled on. Then came a seething crowd
returning veterans from Waterloo.
We left the room, lacking the killer drive.
The crackling-creaking-rustling quickly stopped.
They'd all returned to their ancestral home.

In time, some trendy so-and-so decreed
(ignoring the past visits of the Thames),
the basement decor needed livening up.
He had it done in smart brown hessian
to show off theatre prints—costume designs
from plays—grey aluminium-framed, for sale.
The Thirties' paintwork was all covered up,
and things got warmer. He'd not bargained for
he insects having his same sense of taste—
brown sacking—just what any roach would love.
They did too. What a Spring they had—up, down
and round about—they even did things by
the cloakroom hatch, rode on velvet jackets,
drowned in gin.

Audiences

The actors, standing in brightness, see just
the first few rows and scatters of faces—
Baroque angels in gilt clouds—where small lights
illuminate the Boxes or bulges
in the Upper Circle's curve.

The ushers, in the dimness, clearly see
the audiences whose tickets they have torn:
the sombre families for Ibsen plays,
sourly old and dressed in musty black,
Equus types—deep into psychology
and bent, tourists who're 'doing' the Royal Court
next week, but don't know what is on, those who
were driven to Shakespeare by exams and seem
relieved to find he's full of dirty jokes,
some who want jam on it—bums, tits *and* culture.
These last come armed with binoculars
(they're more high-powered than opera-glasses)
and sit in the front rows for any play
with nudity or sex.

Those who cleaned up defined the audiences
in other ways—'a filthy lot' for more
old-fashioned plays like *Eden End*—
they all sucked sweets.

Night London

The pubs were out, the evening's takings done,
box office-hatches tightly closed. The girls
and boys of Theatre-land waited for their
release, hustling their patrons to the Strand.
'All out?' the firemen asked, huge padlocks
in their hands. The day's last workers left
by stage doors set in alleyways.
The night began . . .

A steel-blue lightness in the half-dark of
the Charing Cross Road marked the Classics foyer—
all-night horror and coffee—three fifty.
A Chinese usher handed little packs
of sickly shortbread buttons to the queue,
then disappeared behind a hatch to dole
out plastic cups of coffee—frothy pale—
sugar and milk compulsory. Two films
and a reel on in the musty dimness
a ticketless straggler wove the side aisle;
bottles dropped from his sodden carrier-bag.
The balding plush soaked Cyprus sherry up.
A policeman, manoeuvring, got him
by the intact elbow of his pee-stained mac.
The emergency exit's long bolt scraped
on concrete. Lamplight flooded in.

The river wind chilled the brightness of squares
and bridges, lifting the sick garbage smells
from stores and restaurants, drying the grimed dew
of parks and monuments. Next day's papers
lay in the great old stations, fresh with print.
Outside, the streets were bare, light, free,
the Tubes all latticed shut.

The Mirror Crack'd

It was days of filming in the warm sun—
a stately home in Kent—the grass was shorn short
under small fruit trees, the green broken with
heraldic bursts of red clover, self-heal
and yellow bird's foot trefoil. Some cows
looked on across a fence.

One time the locals descended, spoiling
shot after shot, standing in the foreground
in their non-Fifties polyester frocks,
before they got down to the autographs.

'Please sign my book for me, Miss Taylor.'
Five minutes later they were round again.
'Can't remember if I asked you,' one woman said.
'I've just done Angela Lansbury. If not, please sign.'

The woman called her husband up to look.
'Ooh, isn't she beautiful?' They peered closely.
She sat motionless on a wooden bench,
her violet chiffon dress caught on splinters.

The man stood thinking. His belly peeped
from a small tear in his orange nylon shirt
close by her face. 'Nah!' he said. 'Take off
all that powder and paint and she'd be just
like you or me.' He rammed his cap down hard
on his oiled hair and went off comforted.

Merging

In *Dogs of War* a Cockney extra gave me
some good tips for survival.

'Never put yourself forward,' he advised.
'We're in it just to be anonymous—
the more so, the better.' He'd merged enough,
he said, to fill the place of umpteen men
on the Titanic's decks, 'Crew, passengers,
waiters, the ruddy lot!' Eventually,
some young assistant sussed him out and pulled
him from behind the bar, saying: 'I never want
to see that ugly mug of yours again!'

'Just mingle, join any queue you see—
it's probably for grub . . .'—not quite such good
advice. Getting in line, I thought for tea,
I nearly got myself stuck with a beard
in *Reds*. His mingling, on the other hand,
brought him an extra day in some beer ad.
They left him gilded in an anteroom,
(one rower too many for the quinqereme),
to mind the others' clothes—he only had
a loincloth on—forgotten, sweating gold, alone.

I've seen him since, I think, merging in films,
tucked away, round the corner from a set,
in Pinewood selling watches from a case.
I saw his brawny arm at Shepperton
amongst an octopus of hands stealing
the cream cakes from a tray while other men
confused the cook with change. And he was one
of six who leaned a table down,
left three accountants grovelling on the ground
for cash and chits, and took us into more
paid overtime.

Man, Woman and Superman

We were working in a cold November,
one night at Pinewood, on *Superman II,*
shivering in our thin, summer clothing
as the wind whistled through the open set.
Between the takes, like moths, we huddled to
the fake-warm brightness of the lights.
A gust of rain, and Superman, legs tweely crossed
in tights, et cetera, opened his brolly.
The assistants ran here and there, voices
scrambled impossibly through megaphones,
the two-way radios at their belts gave out
new orders, talking at cross purposes.
Soon after, silence. Some men descended
from scaffolding to blow up brand-new cars
(parts all screwed loose). On pain of dismissal
we kept our faces solemn—not a smile.
The unit's chip-van soon joined in with flames
(unplanned). A dark, unholy incubus
of black, oiled soot wound from its roof before
a dull explosion. Coughing and choking
we crowded the Daily Planet's office.

You don't talk a lot on a noisy job
like that—nor in the rush to cash your chits.
Weeks on, I heard how one man fell that night—
his heart. He'd faked his age to get the call.
The others, laughing, unaware, passed round
a photo of a man dubbed 'Supercock'
(twenty-eight inches of it, so they said).
The women speculated on its use—
lovemaking Pyramus-and-Thisbe style—
pictured him trousered from the Isle of Man.
The men, while saying it must be a fake,
still thought that one like that would be most prized.

I class it as an extra's legend with
the one about the fat, old 'crowd artiste'
who wet her costume on the Titanic
and got the sack. (She also, it is said,
pulled up her skirts and showed a rural scene
to some director who'd offended her
the film was *Dragonslayer*.)

When Superman and all the rest had gone
that night, it's said, a cunning thief crept through
Metropolis, and, opening all the doors,
took the prams out of Mothercare and filled
them full of videos from the other shops.

1984

We Party Members stood and cheered Big Brother
on Victory Square in 1984.
A smiling soldier, imaged on two screens,
worked his way down a line of hostages,
blowing their heads off like ripe melons.
We applauded him and raised our arms
in a diaphragm-wrenching crossed-fist salute.

A gangway was cleared through the crowd. Lorries
edged forward on their caterpillar tracks
across the mud. Inside were prisoners.
The Asian extras stood, feet bare
on the cold metal of the Army vans,
their legs in irons. We'd seen them painted by girls
squeezing their blood make-up from small foil tubes.
We'd queued with them for soup. And we cried out
'Kill! Kill! Death! Death!' through many takes. We stood
close in the pre-dawn chill and met their eyes
each time the trucks stopped by the mass gallows.

At first light it was all over. Faces
relaxed.The boiler-suits and heavy boots
were handed back to the Wardrobe.
Victims and oppressors, one in acted hate,
were paid the same.

Bond Girl

Back in my extra days, someone once swore
she'd seen me in the latest James Bond film.
I tried to tell her that they only hired
the really glamorous leggy types for that.
(My usual casting was 'a passer-by'.)

I've passed the lot in Pinewood Studios.
It's factory-like, grey aluminium, vast
and always closed. Presumably that's where
they smash up all the speedboats, cars and bikes
we jealous viewers never could afford.

I quite enjoyed the books. Ian Fleming wrote well.
I could identify a touch with Bond,
liking to have adventure in my life.
The girls were something else. All that they earned
for being perfect samples of their kind—
black, Asian, white, blonde, redhead or brunette,
groomed, beauty-parlourised, pleasing in bed,
mixing Martinis that were shaken not stirred,
wearing pearl varnish on their nails not red—
was death. A night (or two) with 007,
then they were gilded till they could not breathe,
chucked to the sharks, shot, tortured, carried off
or found, floating face downward in a pool.

Old Extras

Old extras never die or get the sack,
they simply go on file for horror films—
or so I was told in all seriousness
by a woman on *Tale of Two Cities*,
part of the Old Bailey mob, or, as one
assistant phrased it, (fearing the Union),
'Gallery personnel'.

As we sat in waist-crushing, hessian skirts,
hair under foul mob-caps, she told us how
she'd been put on that file—'just by mistake',
and gone to Central Casting, hair fresh-dyed,
proffering new photos, begging 'Take me off.'
It worked. Now she was saving all the cash
for a good face-lift—one thousand pounds.
She looked all right to me, no real wrinkles
at forty odd, the only obvious flaw—
the ripple of a lousy nosejob.

Lying

One of the sex manuals we swapped at school
decreed the husband should not kiss his wife
in the final stages. The theory was
that women choose to fantasise about
some handsome star and not the bloke they're with.
His face too near to theirs might bring them back
to grim reality and thus prevent orgasm.

Their men are vibrators with pay cheques,
brainless,feelingless fucking posts, engines.
These dutiful wives will stoke their boilers
and fill their tanks to keep them running. Then,
they're faithful in their fashion to Paul Newman
when the lights go out and the lying begins.

It seems okay to want to shut pain out.
When I was tipped back in the dentist's chair,
I sent myself to a Baroque theatre,
amongst gold, white and blue decorations
to the music of Mozart, as his drill
screamed clumsily on a back tooth. It would
seem positively perverse to savour
moments like that and feel them as they are.
But *pleasure*? How can they close off like this,
never experiencing the nuances
of individual feeling and technique,
not seeing the only point of being there
was wanting each other more than the rest
for that short time—lying till sex becomes
duty, a daily pinta, Sunday joint
or yearly jab?

One wife I knew fancied Stewart Granger,
forever 'Scaramouche' buckling a swash.
(Do older ones think necrophiliacly
of Douglas Fairbanks Senior and John Gilbert?)
Her husband, she said, still didn't love her
in spite of her 'bat's hole'. (She'd had their kids
by Caesarian to keep it small.) At night,
he'd lie crying to himself and wanking,
muttering some other woman's name.

Girlie Mags

I do not care a toss if blokes must look
at glossy, big-boobed photos of bad girls.
I've met some centre-stapled, double spreads
who laughing took the cash and went their ways.
Women cannot afford to turn work down.
But how I hate the letters in those mags:
A. had her nipples pierced, linked with a chain,
B. had the firm's alsatian yet again,
C., buggered by six fellas, felt no pain,
and all loved it. So the male bastards claimed,
signing their missives with sweet female names.
All right, my guess is good as theirs,
I'll write and sign the thing John Smith.
Last week I put my bollocks through a mangle,
and loved it. May I recommend?

Sex Objects

I learned from a friend's porno mag that men
can buy the better class of plastic doll,
(posh ones are hard and unyielding, not the
pneumatic sort that fly from windows when
they're pricked), in slow instalments, torso first.

Well-qualified in wanking, Mark saves up
his pennies till they grow to pounds and then
invests in Ingrid, just the body, for
his carnal press-ups—a bit too flesh-pink
for human and she sports a ridgy seam
where back meets front. Mark humanises her—
steals her a black lace bra that doesn't fit,
(he's not that used to seeing naked tits),
and puts a cover of a Cosmo girl
up on the pillow where his doll's neck ends.

Six months on, tired of screwing her pink trunk,
he spends his pocket money on a head.
A bald one comes by post, mouth a red o.
He buys his girl a man-made fibre wig,
and, graduating to fellation, talks
about her to his friends.

He gets the arms for Christmas and soon gives
his doll a voice, a steamy tape; he's good
at it by now, he thinks, and she should tell
him so. The tape's a great success at first,
until he starts to get the timing wrong,
and Ingrid, moaning says 'It's wonderful'—
after he's gone.

Mark's not a legs-man, so these limbs come last—
a duty—something to hook round his back.
He's shocked when they arrive—one black, one white.
The firm's in liquidation and could just
supply him with the halves of two whole pairs.
(The black's from 'Sonia', another doll.)

That limb cures his Pygmalionitis quite.
He starts to look for human girls to fuck,
but finds they usually need persuasion first,
their fannies aren't so neatly set in front and,
unlike Ingrid, they can criticise.

Trying Too Hard

The fruiterer's son, just old enough to drive,
lined their chrome yellow Citroen with fur.
He stuck it neatly in there piece by piece.
I saw him at it at weekends, lying half-in, half-out,
high on the smell of glue.

And there was dear old Twinkletoes' who lived
just opposite our house in Creffield Road.
He exercised hard for a month—trying
to touch his toes and cycling in the air—
getting in training for some girl. For hours
before she came he moved the furniture,
subdued the cushions, music and the lights,
then gave himself an even closer shave.

We've all laughed ourselves sick at men like these.
Less obviously funny are the types
who fiddle with your fasteners hopelessly
like drunks at night getting a door undone,
who blow in your ear in January,
forgetting that all Nature's doing the same,
who pay over-efficient attention
to your nipples as if they're nuts and bolts
which, once unscrewed, will make you fall apart.

I question the sincerity of lust
that lacks an elementary competence.
Religion's out and fornication's in.
It's fashionable to score. Men must oblige
and overdo us like their aftershave,
patching together their self-images—
a fur-lined car, a body kept in shape,
gnomes on the lawn, a woman in their beds.
Only their clumsiness hints at the truth.

AIDS

Condoms can never save the world from germs —
machines run out of them and chemists close;
a friend blames two abortions on the things;
some funny little foreign ones don't fit;
besides, they're not much use for oral sex.

Evangelists rejoice God's got the gays.
(He's let off lesbians though — and wankers too —
of course, we all know they go blind.)

A dinner-party back I heard it all.
'It came from Haiti where men go with pigs.'
'The CIA invented it in labs
to kill the Reds. There was an accident . . .'
'The Government should shoot the lot of them.'
'It's haemophiliacs that I'm sorry for . . .'
Then some Scots poet did his little piece,
four lines about an AIDS-infected fart.
He'd written it on the way down from Arbroath,
specially for the Hastings Festival,
with one (in grunts) about a spastic boy.

We're all immune (or not) to certain things.
Half of the class gets measles, half does not.
We're all sentenced to death. There's no reprieve.
Whom the gods love die early? Some from AIDS.

Whitelaw's Commission says we 'must be made
to think monogamy's the correct way.'
Mr and Mrs Right have married bliss
(and one point seven kids). The rest of us
must chop and change.

Safe sex? There's no such thing.

How to Become a Handy Man

Fifty per cent are no good with their hands.
They may perhaps rebuild a garden wall,
strip paper, plumb the heating, paint the place,
even knit socks . . . but when it comes to sex . . .

I'v asked men to be gentle in my time—
in fact, I've asked and asked and asked again.
Their second touch is leaden as their first.
What's wrong with them—malice or ignorance?

I shall assume it's just the latter state
and hope that they are willing to be taught.
Touch is a matter of intelligence
and can be learned. Boys who smash toys may yet
become skilled experts in fine porcelain—
in theory, anyway, though I have doubts . . .

First, wash your hands before you lay them on
You think that's obvious? Well, it's not to all.
(Some like to tinker with car engine parts
or strip a bike as foreplay to their sex.)
A black-oiled hand descending on a knee's
unlikely to gain entry higher up.

Now that your hands are clean, consider well
the quality of every part you touch—
know our anatomy as well as yours.
Most of our bones and muscles are the same—
the average woman though's a mite less strong.
Two parts are where the crucial difference lies—
the genitals and chest—ours aren't as hard.

I'll give some hints on how to touch those parts.

Our breasts are soft and tender as your balls—
think how you'd like those twisted, bitten, pinched,
given Chinese burns or kneaded viciously.
You're wincing? Seems you get the picture now.
Nipples when treated gently will erect.

See also that your hands are soft enough.
A skin like sandpaper spoils a caress—
a calloused hand rasps like an emery board.

When you have worked your way down to the cunt—
remember fingers are a second best
and not adapted for a macho thrust
unlike your prick they've got bones, knuckles, nails.

Men who have read too many manuals
(written by men) and fancy their technique,
soon move to playing hunt the private parts,
usually with a running commentary.
'Ah yes,' they gloat, 'I've found your clitoris!'
(with pompous satisfaction in the voice).
We don't dare laugh of course—they've got tight hold . . .
OK, a little stimulation's fine
and gets to most. Too much is numbing though—
never get zealous with a clitoris.
These days, the better-read in porno mags
look for a G-spot too, to try their worst.
(Look for? They'd need a bloody periscope!)

Men, if you'd touch us deeply, empathise.
Be in your mind on the receiving end—
the body weight aligned behind your hands,
the hardness or the softness of your skin,
the depth of pressure of fingers and thumbs—
know as you're known, feel all as we feel all.

There are two types of touch (take my advice)—
the nice and nasty. Choose the gentle kind.
The other sort's for sadists or for fools.

Laryngitis

I usually shun doctors (for you don't
know where their hands have been, though you can guess;
and surgeries are full of the diseased.
The coughers all have flu and bronchitis,
the scratchers rashes, but the silent ones
worry me most—they could have anything).
Once, struck with a sore throat, I went to one.
I'd overworked my voice—one scream too much.
He told me to shut up for two whole weeks.

And so I was struck dumb—a sore trial
for a woman of my disposition—
reduced to a toneless whisper, I, who
had leant backwards to kiss the Blarney Stone
and could argue the pants off anyone,
dialectically-speaking. (At school
I had a running bet that I could keep
the RK teacher talking every week
on esoteric points of doctrine I'd
cooked up. I even once conspired to make
all the Old Testament prophecies fit
Judas, not Jesus, like a glove.)

A fortnight on, I returned gladly
to my old ways, talking through half the night,
yelling, screaming and belting out high notes,
ventriloquising speeches for my cats,
laughing uproariously. Two weeks of quiet's
enough for anyone. In Writing, though,
the Chirons and Demetriuses who rule
would make of me a dumb Lavinia.

A dissident citizen of the world,
no country opens up its arms to me.
Woman is often rendered silent,
her greatest shout defined as stridency,
the whisper of her presence hardly heard.

Penis Envy

Freud, you were right! I must expose my id
And show the penis-envy that lies hid.
It's not that I admire the look as such,
It seems a strange adornment for a crutch,
Like sets of giblets from a butcher's shop,
Two kidneys with a chicken-neck on top,
Floating serene in baths like lug-worm bait,
Or, jokily bobbing with the jogger's gait.
Fig-leaves, I'm sure, are prettier far than cocks,
And only suffer greenfly not the pox.
As tools, pricks really aren't reliable,
One minute hard, the next too pliable.
If I had bought a hammer or a chisel
As changeable, I'd think it was a swizzle.

It's not that I'm against them in their place,
But simply that I cannot see a case
For cocks to be a sort of union card
In life's closed shop. I think it very hard
That humans with these fickle bits and bobs
Are given a fairer lot and better jobs.
If only I'd had one of them, it seems
I could have had success, fulfilled my dreams.
A female eunuch though, all I'll attain
Is Pyrrhic victory and trifling gain.

Memo from a Muse

I'll play White Goddess to your Robert Graves,
And place you highest on my list of slaves.
Make me the subject of a vilanelle,
A rondeau and a triolet as well,
An epigram, a ballad or a sonnet;
Make me a pedestal and I'll stand on it.
But girls who darn your Y-fronts can't inspire
Your latest ode, or move your muse's lyre.
I've burnt my bra, but I'll not burn my boats.
I want no husband, I've not sown my oats.
I'd choose an undomesticated life;
It's easier being a goddess than a wife.
No, Poet, I'll not share your humble garret,
I'm your Dark Lady, not Elizabeth Barrett.

Marital Advice

Bride, rule your husband well from the first day—
Don't sew, sweep, cook or serve in any way.
Leave all the chores to males, who do them best—
As all the works of literature attest,
Witness Sam Weller, Sancho Panza, Jeeves
And Puss-in-Boots, the best of feline thieves.
But though you never should wash clothes or dishes,
Comply at once with his less irksome wishes—
Hang naked from the beams or dress in frills,
In leather, fur or net, keep up the pills.
Make him recall this country at its greatest
Was ruled by women, dressed in Britain's latest,
Not fools who burned the cakes or lost their heads,
Or sired stray bastards in soft feather beds.

High noon in the Oral Office

'It's time for a snack!' the President drawled
As he savoured his cigar,
Hand-rolled and flavoured with woman,
As all the best ones are.
It was noon in the Oval Office,
The intern was standing by,
Her dress was half-unbuttoned,
Her skirts were riding high.
The President talked on the telephone,
Discussing matters of state,
While the intern tucked into his lunchbox,
And ate and ate and ate.
The hot dog squirted and stained her dress—
'Get it cleaned!' the President said,
But she put it by for a rainy day,
Took the man to the cleaners instead.
Keep salami for home consumption,
Feed your interns on caviar—
It's cheaper than sharing your lunchbox—
And smoke, don't suck your cigar.

Advice to Champagne Charlies

If you'd sup bubbly from a shoe,
Remember certain types won't do.
Who'd raise a pensioner's Aqua Skips,
Filled with lost corn pads, to their lips,
Or farmyard wellies caked with mire,
Last used when mucking out the byre?
Who'd crave a sip from hippies' sandals,
Steel-capped boots off kicking vandals,
Lambskin-lined, hand-stitched moccasins,
Crepe-soled shoes worn by assassins?
Doc Martens taste a little strong;
Hush Puppies have a canine pong;
And every athlete's trainers stink—
The Odoreaters spoil your drink.
Sling-backs, flip-flops, Scholls and sneakers
Don't hold much, for all are leakers.
Tap shoes leave a metallic taste.
Also avoid the fur-encased
And slippers trimmed with maribou,
Unless you wish to sup fluff too.
And think what scrubbers wear stilletoes
To teeter through the King's Cross ghettoes!
The hygiene-conscious should shout: 'Pass!'
Or stick to Cinderella's glass.
But I like quantity, the shoes I'd choose
Are pantomime size twenty-twos.

Country Walk

I went into the countryside for a walk
and took some bread for the ducks
and my camera to take photographs.
As I carefully shut the farm gate
the old bull said: 'Leave that open, Missus,
I want to see that heifer next door
last time she had a headache.'
I went to the pond and threw bread to the ducks:
'Stuff your Mother's Pride' they said,
'We wants worms.' I put up my camera
to take a picture of a nest,
and the birds said:
'God damn that voyeur, let's crap on her lenses.'
I sat down for my picnic.
There was a little hedgehog nearby.
I undid my thermos and poured him some milk.
And the hedgehog said, 'Keep your filthy cow-muck,
I haven't got stomach ulcers. What I want
is your pin-cushion for a dildo.'

The Serpent's Complaint

One day I heard a serpent hiss,
'To think that it has come to this!
I saw a simple rustic pair
In Eden's garden, loafing there.
I gave them luscious fruit to taste
And taught them how to be unchaste.
But am I thanked? Oh, no, not I.
They just increase and multiply,
And blame each sin and bad mistake
Upon this well-intentioned snake.
Without my aid life would have been
A dreary pious rural scene—
No playing cards, no port with Stilton,
No Bosch, no Dante, no John Milton.

Goat Show

The show was due to start at two o'clock;
one judge, white-coated, entered up some names;
a tousled Toggenburg and herd looked on.
The owner, rumpled as his goat, had two
grey upright feathers in his hat, like horns.
Some half hour late, the others came along—
large spotted Anglo-Nubians, Saanens,
blow-dried white kids, another Toggenburg.
The first, bored to malevolence, shat round.
Her class was next (a second out of two).
Her bloke, disconsolate, questioned the judge
and went off scratching his short beard. The rest
stood round in groups or knelt on half-bald knees
stained by the grass. The Anglo-Nubians
posed like a nest of tables by the ropes.
I sat down on the only patch of turf
left currant-free. A chocolate kid crept up,
fresh from undoing someone's Indian skirt,
and kissed me just like Andrew Marvell's nymph's
young fawn—a pleasant moment till I saw
it press its tender lips against the bold
triangularly-folded rectums of
its peers. 'She's been so good,' her mistress said.
'It's her first show.' Eight classes on, after
some small resentments, almost every goat
has a rosette—red, blue or green. Four wait
for 'Best in Show', ('Reserve Best', too,
a category that's seldom found in life).
'This year', one owner whispers gratefully,
'they didn't pick up his receding chin.'

Guide Dog

On Wednesdays in St Leonards, by the shops,
a wicked guide dog leads her master wrong.
The man is doubly blind, quite unaware
hes being kept waiting by each empty road.
'Come on,' he says to her gently, 'Come on!'
attributing the knocks and bumps he gets
to the crass carelessness of passers by.
His smiling golden retriever leads him on
through various talking groups, then stops for fleas,
or tramps him off the kerb and into shit.
Nobody dares to interfere.

It's like some marriages—you just can't say
'That bitch has led you up the garden path!'
Some wives or husbands quite enjoy the times
their pompous partners put a foot in it.
There's not much harm in that. More sinister,
some watch like spiders for the other's end.
After my father's death, my mother found
envy, not pity, in most women's eyes.

One day, perhaps, I'll hear a screech of brakes
and see the blind man overtaken,
the hand that held her harness lightly, broken,
a day-glow band still wrapped around his arm,
the dog, a Levite, on the other side,
preening to take another owner in.

The Fear of Splitting Up

I've always had a horror of the splits,
though flexible enough in other ways—
the lotus is no problem and I can sing
and drink water, standing on my head.

Though I'd not advocate a lifestyle where
my legs were never the least bit apart—
the fear of splitting up will always stop
me half a dozen inches from the ground.

I could just see myself like some old peg,
a scissors that has lost its middle screw,
or Mistress Jekyll and old Mother Hyde—
two halves apart leading their different lives.

Fortune

Jehovah, Jupiter or Lady Luck,
deal me an ace, roll me a double six.
Life's odds are stacked without a little help.

A crooked croupier's rigged the roulette wheel.
The dice are cogged. The cards are thumbed and marked.
I've watched the game, seen other players' hands—
more royal flushes than a palace lav.

What law dictates the disposition of luck?
Returns for seeds sown in a previous life?
The favour of the Gods? A devil's pact?

Jehovah, Jupiter or Lady Luck,
deal me an ace, roll me a double six.

I Could Use a Butt of Canary

And now the battle of the bards ensues
For which of us should follow after Hughes.
My early poems were historical,
From factual to allegorical.
Although I've tried all forms and served my time
In different metres, not to mention rhyme,
I've read the cuttings and am sad to see
No journalists have nominated me.
I feel they see me as the worst of wasters
And give their backing to bland poetasters.
Yet early laureates were satirical,
With biting wit, not merely lyrical.
Jonson wrote up a voyage down a sewer
And Dryden's plays could titillate the viewer.
And as for Shadwell—what a mucky sod!
(The cleaner Cibber wrote like Policeman Plod.)
I don't regret the seventeenth century wage,
Fixed at the rate it was in Jonson's age,
For I'm quite partial to Canary wine—
An annual butt of it would go down fine.
(I heard that Ted insisted on his dues
And had it bottled up marked *Chateau Hughes*).

Bird Watching

Bad men, it's said, behave 'like animals'.
(If beasts should ever imitate mankind
we'd never call our lives our own again.)

Next life, I'm going up the social scale.
Four feet? Too risky! Men might have my hide.
A bird? No chicken though—they're factory-farmed.
I'll settle for a gull's life by the sea.

My first few years, a dopey speckled thing
with sloe-black eyes and long St.Trinian's legs
like wrinkled stockings with brown leather feet,
I start by picking mussels from the beach
and bathe in boating lakes among my kind.
Then, growing bolder, I will leave my home
to fly from coast to coast, try city life
and feast on junk, join ferries bound for France
or ride the thermals high above the cliffs.

At five, with all my childhood freckles gone,
demure in white and grey, I seek a mate
bigger and stronger, but much like myself,
with kind, straw-coloured eyes as mild as mine,
an orange beak and long thin, clapper-tongue,
a deep pink throat that opens roaring wide
for bleakly-operatic Cockney cries.

I keep my head down when I see the gull
I want (males like that act). Convinced I'm not
a threat, he lets me move into his pad.

In Spring, I lead him on with cooing cries.
He says sex feels like flying on my back.

He takes his turn upon our clutch of eggs
and feeds me while I'm housebound—that's his job.

We kick the heads of humans who come near.
I test this mate of mine—if he protects
our mutual investment, then I'm his
for life. Divorce looms otherwise . . .

Our marriage, made in heaven, seems to last
no money problems, mortgage, DIY—
the roof we share never cost us a cent.
Our nest's a mess, but we don't care a toss.
We're out a lot, you see. Our kids are fine—
a little stupid, true—but they will learn.
Our sons can fly at least—well, just about.
It's time they left. It's time we were alone.

This incarnation round I feed four gulls.
They breakfast shortly after dawn each day.
The males knock on my window with their beaks.
While I look out at them, the birds look in.

Next time, when I become a herring-gull,
I hope to keep some data in my head . . .
Charm humans and make friends of them.
Councillors order culls, believing gulls
will multiply by two by two by two:
endear yourself to those who'll make a fuss
about the 'sacredness of life' and tell
those nincompoops no creature breeds to form
and there are casualties from storms and oil.
Charm humans, but don't get *too* close to them . . .
Keep off their runways and their aeroplanes,
don't tread on glass, be careful of their tips,
eschew the plastic from their packs of beer

and never catch their tit-bits in your beak—
just let them drop—then look before you eat.

Men

I sing of Men—crude, thoughtless, kinky men.

The ones who recommend you to a mate
and bring him round—fat, ugly, hopeful too.
('But why object? He only wants to watch
well, for the first ten minutes, anyway . . .')

Those who are grieved you're not a lesbian;
they'd bargained on two girls to fill their bed.

The guilty types who ask to be abused—
I'll swear alright, but in my own good time—
or leave, muttering, 'Sorry about last night.'

Each who, unwisely seeks comparisons,
needs constant humouring like a lunatic,
wants A-plus marked in teacher's big black book.

Last, those who in the throes of passion drop
your clothes, then, stop to hang their trousers up.

There's nothing *badly* wrong with blokes like these—
they wouldn't use you as a punching-bag
or ask to have their faces shat upon—
a Civil Service taste I heard from some
Madame's good friend. All that they need to make
them perfect men is some *good* woman's love.
I'm glad that I am not that sort.

Married Men

These married men . . .

The average, straight, uncomplicated type
shifts his ring over to the right, pops round
the corner in a pub to use the phone,
tells her he's doing overtime again,
tells you he'd gone to pee.

Others like to lie solely to themselves—
get you to ring, or press you to their cheek
so they can tell their wives quite truthfully:
'I never kissed her, she kissed me. In fact,
she did it several times.'

The candid take you back to meet their worse
or better halves, take the Director's chair,
set up an ad lib drama in the home.

Just Good Friends

I'm the 'just friendship' one,
the other Other Woman in his life.
I get to hear about the other two.

He says his wife's too old at 45
for sex. He has a girl of 24 for that.
He calls her 'brainless'—she forgets the Pill.
He jokes about leading her on to try
odd kinks that make her look ridiculous.

I'm told he's never mixed friendship and sex.
His wife like me's a friend. They haven't had
much sex and none of it was any good.
She doesn't clean the place or cook for him,
or put a penny into paying bills.
'I run a one-man charity,' he says.
She doesn't care a fuck about his work.
She's scratched his face, given him various knocks,
torn a review-copy to little bits,
plays rather funny little jokes on him
like lying round pretending to be dead.
Last time he told me problems on the phone
I heard her yelping like a terrier.
'She's frigid,' he says.

The roofing bloke he paid to stay with her
and do the roof while he was off with Mum
was just 'a friend'. The roof still leaks.
The man with a tattoo across his face
who turned up in their bedroom once, was just
'a friend'. She goes to several private views a night,
tells him she's off to use a word-processor
(belonging to a friend) at 1 a.m.

He thinks that I should give up 'using men',
in fact, give them all up, just be his friend.
He talked of *Brief Encounter* in the pub.
I'm his 'white kitten' too. We're just good friends.
I'm welcome in his house to stay the night.
(I'll take a rain-check on that though—for fear
of meeting tattooed men.)

What do I hang on for? The 'Love' he puts
upon the letters that he sometimes writes?
The 'Love and admiration' on his books?
The sighing pauses on the telephone?
His hand upon my cheek, his lips on mine?
Blue eyes? He's quite a handsome shit.

Censorship

The BBC does not like certain words.
Dildoes and buggery are always out.
'Cocks are OK, as long as they aren't sucked!'
a young researcher telephoned me back.

Latin's polite. Vagina just meant sheath.
What doctors use, of course, must be all right.
(But penis was a penis—nothing else.
The Romans liked to call a prick a prick.)

The BBC's De-effer bleeps things out
or else suggests a synonym instead.
A poet I know was told he should use screw—
his line—'There's fuck-all fucking in the grave.'

I got away with using bugger once.
I tried to be demure at first and said
it rhymed with Rum Tum Tugger, but the host
coerced me to recite it at the end.

In Wales, I said a simple 'prick' and 'piss'—
the show's producer had okayed both words,
but when the bosses' switchboard jammed with calls,
her earphone buzzed 'For God's sake, get her off!'

These days, when on the air, I just conform
and skirt around like the professionals,
so audiences can play a crossword game:
'Four letters, sounds like duck, begins with F'.

That Word

'I bet you're glad your daughter wasn't here
tonight to hear that word,' I heard one man
say to another man the night I read.
His hair looked dyed. His face was red with rage
which made the bird tattoo flying down his neck
seem extra blue.

I rather wondered if he and his friend
that-worded their own daughters at weekends.
Statistics prove lots of men do.

A vicars girl taught all the class that word
when I was nine. I really took to it—
so easy to remember and pronounce
and good for rhymes. It's not a synonym—
an honest word that only means one thing.
I've used it ever since. Beside all that,
I rather like the short, sharp shock it gives
to men with daughters to protect.

Mills and Boon

The Midlands Arts Centre in Birmingham
hosted a lecture for the Festival,
on Mills and Boon.

An editress and author gave a talk,
like two American evangelists.
We Moonies sat there drinking it all in.
Too many Regency, too few Renaissance men —
they're slightly short of costume romance plots.
These days the heroines are allowed careers;
Doctor and Nurse can now be Doc plus Doc.
We were advised to study lots of books
before we sent in our first manuscript.
(Aha, I thought, you've got the innocents —
housewives who want a gentle mental-wank,
so now you're going round the festivals
to rope in more pretentious literary shites.)
They'd have us all reading and writing the stuff.

Their table had three piles beside the jugs.
One handout told us how to type our book —
some useful tips — like numbering from 1.
Another said what contents were allowed.
The third was just a little order form
for the cassette.

Then came the question-time — a welcome break.
A fattish person in the top back left
wanted to know why they'd rejected hers
when she had followed every single rule
and women's magazines just loved her stuff.

Others showed much willingness to set to work,
queried the pay. (They didn't get to know.)
The local author though dropped subtle hints —

she had a word-processor and microwave
and now was 'one-up in the housing-chain'.
Some asked what sort of girl . . . what sort of man.
All sounded Saved as Billy Graham's flock.
I meant to be a Devil's advocate
and said I didn't like their brutal males.
The author told me she'd had 'thirty-seven
affairs' with them—the people in her books.
An addict zombie murmured fervently,
'My neighbour lent me a whole pile of them
(I was in plaster to the hip) I thought
the heroes were all *lovely* men.'
I was outnumbered evidently.
The editress intent on winning my soul—
she saw me as an author for her lot—
took it I didn't like this modern sex,
and told me a nice old scenario
about a widower with two small kids
who slept rooms from his bride on The First Night.
I had to say 'Perhaps he was impotent
and doped her cocoa just to cover up.'
She didn't like my theory all that much.

We should be careful what we fantasise—
it might, it really might come true at last.
I've tried to see myself within those books.
'Mills and Boon heroines don't sleep around,'
we'd heard. 'They're 17 to 28.'
None of that audience even qualified.

I'm more the hero type, I'd have to say:
tall, dark and handsome, powerful (if not rich).
I should get some young, trembling, virgin bloke,
crush him against a wall in a hotel
(in some exotic spot) and bruise his lips.

Then, chapters on, after an argument,
I'd dominate him in the lift, get one
strong hand inside his silken shirt and tear
the buttons off—no hassle, he can sew.
I'd feel his nipples harden at my touch.
The other hand would grasp his slender nape.
I'd press against him with my powerful frame.
His mouth would open slowly under mine.
(He'd feel exquisite torture all the while.)
In the last chapter when things are resolved,
I'd scoop him up and chuck him on the bed.
(My art school days and frequent DIY
have made me quite exceptionally strong.)
He'd smell the perfume of a thousand flowers—
he'd know I'm single, know that I'm his boss.
As I bore down, I'd hear his 'Show me how . . .
But no, I've got it wrong it's 'We must wait!'
'Show me how' is only for The Wedding Night.
The virgin bloke's a mercenary bitch.

Death of a Princess

We felt we knew her better than ourselves—
On books and newspapers, in every guise,
Her face beamed down from supermarket shelves;
We read the gossip, lapped up all the lies.
Wife, mother, supermodel, saint or star?
We plainer, older mortals shed a tear,
Our fantasies died with her in that car.
Conscious of our own frailty, we felt fear.
Another forty years, or just a day?
We cannot really choose the *when* or *how*—
Snuffed out in the fast lane, Diana's way,
Or lingering upon some hospice bed,
(Without the thought of her to visit now).
The life of each of us hangs by a thread.

Song of the Nymphomaniac

From Baffin Bay down to Tasmania
I've preached and practised nymphomania,
Had gentlemen of all complexions,
All with varying erections:
Coalmen, miners, metallurgists,
Gurus, wizards, thaumaturgists,
Aerial artists, roustabouts,
Recidivists and down-and-outs,
Salesmen, agents, wheeler-dealers,
Dieticians, nurses, healers,
Surgeons, coroners and doctors,
Academics, profs and proctors,
Butchers, bakers, candle-makers,
Airmen, soldiers, poodlefakers,
Able seamen, captains, stokers,
Tax-inspectors, traders, brokers,
Preachers, canons, rural deans,
Bandy cowboys fed on beans,
Civil-servants, politicians,
Taxidermists and morticians.
I like them young, I like them old,
I like them hot, I like them cold.
Yet, I'm no tart, no easy lay—
My name is Death. We'll meet one day.

The After Life

No sex hereafter—oh, what tosh—
Hell's one large Soho run by Bosch.
He's Master of the Revels here,
Giving the Damned what they prefer:
Rent an empusa for the day,
Or Satan whose dick's cold, they say.
Straight sex in Hell is infra dig—
So choose a mermaid or a pig,
Then do it standing on your head,
Or use a duck's back as a bed.
Experiment with every vice—
Remember, God can't damn you twice!

Crap Literature

I have this penchant for crap literature—
a sort that's rarely kept by booksellers.
I've had finds in jumble sales and rescued
recherché items out of skips.

We think we know it all now, and banish
our far-flung ideas from this world into Space.
I like the creatively preposterous
Edwardians who had no such inhibitions
and built unique arch-villains with panache
The Strand Magazine's beautiful doctor,
one of whose crimes involved a vase breaking
on a note of a tune she had written,
Gaston Leroux's convict, Cheri-Bibi,
who swapped his face by plastic surgery
(without an anaesthetic's aid) for that
of the fiancé of the girl he loved,
Guy Boothby's torturing Doctor Nikola,
appearing in China, Tibet, London
and Italy, burning herbal truth drugs
or killer incense in his shrine.

I love the strange interiors—not plush,
mahogany or sepia-tinted prints,
piano-legs dressed up in knicker-frills—
Le Queux's anarchist safe-houses
full of bombs, severed heads and automata,
Pemberton's island cities, copper-covered ships.

Some thrillers blind us with their science.
The World's Finger shows crime-solving at its best—
the victim's eyeball, properly cut out,
reveals the killer on the retina.

Others I like for their sheer messiness.
Take the example of *The Devil's Die.*
Three men in love with the same girl. The one
who gets her then decides to bump her off
and gives her cholera, although they sleep
in the same bed. He gets it too and dies.
She cracks up. Meanwhile, in the USA,
the other two get premonitions and
turn back, lost in the Sage Brush on the way.
(The locals hadn't liked the look of them.)
Mohammed Ali, an Indian doctor
(who being black is not allowed to get
the girl) saves his young artist friend for her
by filling his pith-helmet with marrow
cracked from dead buffaloes' bones.

Double Act

There's a new way of making love around.
An Ancient Greek, some say, invented it.
He practised daily by a mountain pool.
But Englishmen have since perfected it
and passed the art through every public school.

First, stand and face your partner. Take your time.
Undress him with your eyes. Admire each part.
Smooth back your hair and smile seductively.
He's happy too. See how he smiles at you.
He's pleased. You're pleased. So give yourself a hug.
Tell him he's exquisite and blow a kiss.
He'll blow one back—you're really synchronised,
a perfect pair—no worse or better half.
Whatever he does, simply do the same.
He's waiting for it, morning, noon and night,
in bedrooms, bathrooms, cloakrooms and hotels.
Instant demand—he's ready when you are.
He's hooked. You're hooked. The act is ecstasy—
no nasty body fluids, no disease—
pure pleasure with the one you really love.

Carnal Conversation

'Now I was really raped,' a fat man said
to his fat friend walking through the Old Town
in Hastings, the day of the Carnival.
'And I mean really raped,' he said. 'Last night.'

They stopped and he said it again outside
the little joke shop that sells 3-cupped bras
(marked 'For the woman who has everything')
beside false lips and 'Sexy Cucumbers'
(these obviously unscrew for batteries)
small packs of fart powder and 'Mucky Pups'.

Well, maybe he was telling the world the truth,
if she was big enough to drag him off
and knock him down, undo his zip and fall
on the erection he just happened to have.

Dildoes

Dildoes—they come in varied size and shape—
five foot, five six, six foot, fair, middling, dark.

Is it too much to ask for brains as well
as balls? Okay, I've had my share of thrills—
the times when everything's well choreographed.
I put my glass down as we start to kiss;
nothing is spilt; our fastenings all undo
and everything comes off; our heights match well;
I fit him like a glove.

Yet I feel trapped in some dark sci-fi film.
My task, it seems, is sussing robots out.
They look so human it's quite hard to tell
until the things go on about their cars
or use the same set piece to chat you up.
(The one part they can't simulate's the mind.)

Some leave the works in a half-programmed state—
these are the easiest ones to spot—I saw
a cheap Italian model in South Ken,
'Disco?' it went, then, 'Whisky—vodka—rum—
bacardi—coke?' and, 'Fucky-fucky in hotel?'
'No thanks!' I said. Its batteries ran down.

I think I'm still a virgin mentally.
I'm thirty-one, I've had no real man.
I'd like to, though, just for the novelty.

The Book Trade

Mike's seen my photo in a magazine
and thought it only fair to send me his—
headless with almost all the genitals
modestly covered with a clutched white towel.
Fans spend three ninety-nine and think a book
is not enough for that amount of cash—
the poet's body ought to be thrown in.
This week's free offer? Air miles? Green Shield Stamps?

Well, Mike, though I am not about to be
your 'partner on the swinging couples scene',
I'll spare a little time to talk finance.
Of that three ninety-nine I get a tenth
minus my agent's ten per cent plus VAT;
about a third goes to the bookseller;
the rest of it's the publishers'. By rights,
if anybody should be screwed . . .

Ken Roberts

Ken Roberts rings me up to ask if I
like going to the cinema alone,
and, like a fool, I stop and talk to him.
He says he bets that he could turn me on.
(I bet he can't.) I say this, but it's hard
to put his kind of bubbly pervert down.

Do I enjoy it when a stranger puts
his hand upon my knee during the film?
'No, only old and ugly men do that!' I say.
He tells me that he's 46.

He says he sees me at the kitchen sink
in stockings and a short bright blue silk dress
and slides his hand from stocking-top to thigh.
What would I do? he asks.

'I'd tip my dirty water over you.'
'I think I'd like you doing that,' he says.
'Oh no you wouldn't,' I say, 'it's full of grease
and nasty sticky little bits of food.'
'Oh yes I would!' Ken says.

'Expense of Spirit'

'Shakespeare's a good psychologist!' I'd said,
(the present tense, the man still lives to me)
a casual remark, post-mortemised
by the historian I was talking to.
'He couldn't be. Psychology's a science
that hadn't been invented in his day . . .
Shakespeare showed feeling for his fellow man!'
(He told me what he thought I'd meant to say.)
I felt the sofa wasn't long enough
for both of us and wished he'd go away.

Okay, I know that Shakespeare wasn't a shrink
(more qualified in poaching than exams)
and didn't question people on his couch.
Or, if he did, he wasn't paid for it.
I still maintained that Shakespeare analysed
our motives for each act and wrote that truth.
Clever Dick challenged me to prove that point.
'One line,' he ordered, 'or a part of one'.
A hundred things (and all irrelevant)
went coursing through my mind, like 'Out, damned spot!'
'Then slip I from her bum; down topples she';
I settled for 'men have died from time to time
and worms have eaten them, but not for love'.
Mercifully, he went off to look it up.

Shakespeare wrote many thousand truths—
open the Works at almost any page
(I sometimes use the book for oracles.)
The only line I'd quarrel with's on lust.

Come off it, Shakespeare, lust's a lot of fun.
Like meals, or visits to the theatre,
it's over soon, but leaves good memories.
If thwarted, there's less pain it than love.

Lust is quite practical. (There's plenty more
fish in the sea—if what you fancy's fish.)

Love's complicated—the expensive one.
The thing unbalances, throws judgment out.
Its centring on one and only one
engrosses thought and permeates your life.
We writers, when in love, have twice the work,
rewriting all the damned self-pity out.

All right, I know that love's not terminal.
As a disease, I'd call it chronic, though;
it reoccurs and's hardly curable.
There's nothing to be gained from it, unless,
by some rare chance, it's equal on both sides.
Your line on lust, exactly sums it up . . .
'Expense of spirit in a waste of shame'.

A Curious Hobby

I've trawled the red light districts of the world,
Seen strange things done with goldfish in Japan.
I've watched the sex shows near the Reeperbahn.
(The girls looked bored and never ever smiled.)
In Cairo I went dancing in a club
(15 Israeli firemen were my date).
In Turkey I cross-dressed to enter streets
Where burly men queued up for sex in droves.
I've seen a mirrored brothel in Hong Kong
And sipped cold coffee in an Athens den
Beside a man with pretty little breasts.
I've questioned sex-shop-keepers on their wares.
Some offer videos with titles like:
Blame it on Bambi, *Eels for Pleasure*, *Dicks*.
Others sell dolls for those who have no friends
('Lora who groans and moans and begs for more')
Black rubber whatsits, leather God-knows-whats,
Or gold vibrators and inflating pigs.

The National Health

'When the National Health first started,' he said,
'her brother went and got the lot from them:
glasses for seeing, glasses for reading,
a double set of teeth, a wig, a sponge . . .
And then, he died.'

In Praise of Old Men

Be wise, take up with steady older men—
You'll never feel alone at night again,
With reassuring snores to shake the bed
And sets of teeth to guard beside your head.
They'll pace the corridor at two or three,
Looking for burglars while they're off to pee,
Better than Dobermans, they eat less meat,
Are far less boisterous, never in heat.
And if for steamy atmospheres you'd try,
Just set their thermals by the fire to dry.
And oh, what kinky Kama Sutra games
Are played with rupture belts and Zimmer frames.
In short, I'd say, though staminalessness is hateful,
At least the old Methusalehs are grateful.

Ode to a Fart

When Earth's first human progeny awoke
He looked upon his arse, and lo! it spoke.
Since then, a Babel-multitude of tongues
Sprang up, confusing man, who used his lungs
To breathe, his mouth to speak and soon forgot
His former ways. And yet, his tail was not
Thus to be silenced, but protested on—
A voice that lingers when the spirit's gone,
From zephyrine to dark Satanic call,
A classless critic, understood by all
From Northern navvies fed on mushy peas
To titled schoolboys lurking in the trees.

Rewind

At the end of life, some say that Time runs
Back, fast like a full cassette on Rewind.
Slack tape pulls taut, winds itself neatly till
That click betrays the end and the beginning.
Flat playing fields, short trousers, childhood friends
Track across the mind's eye—a thousand things
Pack those last seconds, like a comic strip—
Splat! Zoom! Ker-pow! Authority is clear,
Man's riddles solved. And in this simpler world
Right stands alone. But we are prey to our
Deceiving senses, dulled by complexity.
Sight of that kind is only given to those
'Sans everything'. We stand bemused outside,
Receiving only the garbled version.

Iconoclasts

'Our baby fucked the Bible!'—boastful Dads
Love to reveal the talents of their lads.
With flexing fingers and a rapist's look,
His little monster grabs their only book.
Genesis, Exodus are soon no more . . .
Leviticus and Numbers hit the floor.
Old and New Testaments are next divorced,
Major and minor prophets rolled and forced
Into his porringer of puréed pear.
He's bored to buggery in his high chair.

Babies are all iconoclasts by will,
But mostly lack the strength to do much ill.
Now get a toddler on to wrecking spines
And you'll be deep in debt with library fines.
Kids roger books—just look at Rupert Bear
And splattered, ravaged annuals everywhere.
Girls' and Boys' Owns and well-shagged Andrew Langs,
Too screwed to salvage, give collectors pangs
And prove Victorian brats were just as bad
'Seen but not heard', they still fucked books like mad.

Water-birth

While pregnant I felt close to Mother Earth
And thought I'd like a New Age water-birth.
I watched the videos and bought the book.
The mothers had an awe-inspiring look—
All so relaxed, they did not scream or yell—
And all their partners were involved as well.
Aromatherapy, candles and flowers
Transformed their 'birthing rooms' and baths to bowers.

Hospital decor is, alas, not chic.
My baby's birth had a more comic streak.
His Dad watched *Dirty Harry* on TV
(For the eighth time) intent on Clint, not me.
I wore a half-inflated rubber duck
(A head rest) round my neck. And by bad luck,
The Mickey-Mouse-shaped lilo sprang a leak—
Too many Mums had chewed on it that week.
Each time it sank, the midwife mended it—
Surgical plasters and her puncture kit.
At last, both head and body were expelled:
Young Alexander shot out, jet-propelled,
A bubble at his mouth like a cartoon.
I sat. They ran the water out, and soon,
He fastened on a tit and drank his fill.
Almost a year since he is on it still!

Placenta Alexander

(named after my son for obvious reasons . . .)

Take some placenta, preferably your own—
You will not find this dish in Delia's book—
Seethe some shallots in butter in a pan,
Add chunks of afterbirth and let it cook.
Pour in some sherry for a richer sauce.
(By now your family will all have fled,
Fearing that they must eat this offal dish.)
Swirl in crême fraiche and serve it on a bed
Of white Basmati rice. Garnish with herbs:
Some coarse chopped lovage, flat-leaf parsley too.
Is it a waste product or human flesh?
Who knows? Who cares! It's very good for you.

Married Bliss

Right up until our wedding day
He did not fart in bed,
But everything got more relaxed
As soon as we were wed.

I felt it rude not to reply
When we were in the sack.
I waited for a year or so,
And then, I farted back.

And now the baby and the cat
Join in our tête-à-tête,
And every night is music night
With the family wind quartet.

Dogs

Young men, like pups, can be somewhat unformed.
Unless you're certain of their pedigree,
it's hard to see how they'll mature and grow.
(Alsatians will fuck dachshunds now and then.)

A man who has some mileage on the clock
in theory would be best. You know the worst—
how much his hair is likely to recede,
his face to fold, as 'character' comes out.
(Furrows look better on the land than skin—
the worst one is a constipated frown—
laughter lines are the most forgivable.)
Auden grew wrinkled as a shar-pei dog.
Most only reach the pug or bloodhound stage.

I've tried 'the older man'—the problem's not
the looks. It's the god-awful temperament.
Rottweiler-grumpiness sets in with age.
I'll stick to pups who're younger than myself—
they've got more stamina for exercise
and better natures, willing to be trained.
I'll whistle and they'll come, fetch, carry, beg.
Of course, I wouldn't take on one too young.
I'd certainly prefer him weaned from Mum.

Old dogs, it's said, cannot be taught new tricks
and those they have are all predictable.
They guard their kennels self-importantly,
mark out their territory in wind and piss,
bark righteously for any trifling cause,
follow the pack in every bloody thing.
All their affection's of the boisterous kind:
they're awfully free with dandruff, spittle, hair.
The eviller ones are snappish with young kids,
chase those who're weaker than themselves (like sheep),

seize you and won't let go, roger your legs,
lose socks, worry old bones and bury things.
And all take leaks at frequent intervals.

Don't get me wrong—I'm partial to a dog.
I blame their breeders for the way they're trained.

Pussy Love

My love, let me tell you about a cat—
black and white moggy, six years old or more,
'No Value' written on the form I signed
before the Cats' Home let me take her off.
I didn't really fall for her at first.
It wasn't instant love, I must confess.
My bed was pussyless. I craved a cat.
I simply felt a need to fill that space.

Brit really worked on me. She purred all week.
A constant friend, she gardened by my side.
A collar of living fur, she'd drape herself
about my neck, or settle on my lap,
to watch my words appear across the screen.
She followed every time I left the house.
I shut her up. She leapt down, ledge by ledge,
until she reached the ground and joined me there.

She tried so very hard to win my heart,
breathing her furry passion in my ear,
rubbing her silkiness against my legs,
pining without me when I went away,
in time I really grew to love that cat.
I talked to her and told her how I felt.
I know she understood. Each word of love
acted upon her like an elixir—
her coat shone iridescent, sparkling black.

My straying days were numbered when you came.
I saw you as the one to set me free.
(Other men had stamped 'No Value' on my form.)
When you were pussyless you sought me out.
(I know that it was little more than that.)
It wasn't instant love for you, but please
give me a chance. I've really tried like Brit.

Love *can* be won. I've learned that much from her.
Meet me halfway in this and pledge me yours,
and I'll forget past grief and shine with hope.

Bed Time

Sex in the afternoon is always good.
It's honest lust, not lodgings for the night;
no one's too drunk or tired to manage it.

The afternoon's discreet, ambiguous,
a time when no excuses need be made.
Each enjoys each—they know as they are known.
There's no concealment—daylight's always on.
And when it's time to leave, the night's still young—
home, food, TV all wait—and best of all,
the peace of being alone in your own bed.
Solitary sleep's less disillusioning.

Night sex is often far less pleasurable—
a tired, furtive, fumbling in the dark.
Objective vision comes with morning's light.
(I have the knack of always waking first.)
I dreamed of friends but find a stranger there—
his mouth gapes snoring wide; yesterday's style,
the careful, blow-dried cut—is now on end;
one duvet-clutching hand has dirty nails;
and, something ludicrous, the modest sod's
managed to get his pants back on in bed.
He wakes and things get worse. I must wipe off
the grin those pants inspired and try to talk.

The in-built problem with a one-night stand
is how to handle things after you've slept.
How many lovers' moods are synchronised?
An early-morning surliness in one
undoes everything tender done or said.
I'd advocate pre- or post-breakfast fucks
to show continuance of last night's desire,
proof positive that neither has regrets.

Morning After

The morning after and there's little left
for either one of you to say.

There's nothing in his rooms. (The coffee that
he'd asked you back to have was never there.)
There's only time enough for him to drive
you into work — his place not yours.

He swears at every passing motorist
along the way, before he stops to put
you down. 'Last night,' he says, 'was . . . interesting.'

And you're left standing there. You notice then
he's dropped you far from where you'd meant to go.

Blow Jobs

You'd get more protein from the average egg;
the taste's a tepid, watery nothingness—
skimmed milk? weak coffee? puréed cucumber?

Fellation's not a woman's idea of fun.
Just doing it as foreplay is okay.
You kiss me, I'll kiss you's a quid pro quo,
but carrying on until the buggers come—
suck, suck, suck, suck for half a bloody hour!
(I haven't timed it but it feels that way.)

There's nothing in the act for us. Our mouths
are better stimulated by a kiss.
The sucked lie back (with beatific smiles),
forget our bodies in their private dreams,
while we grow cold, detached, unloved, untouched,
our heads like 3-D sporrans on their groins,
bored out of mind, with aching jaws and cheeks,
like kids that Santa gave a plastic flute,
still trying to get a tune on Boxing Day.

'Toothless George' sucked all comers to the rocks
in a secluded Jersey cove each June.
(He'd come from Blackpool for his yearly treat.)
Men love the act, sucking and being sucked.
Most women wish they'd keep it to themselves.

No Smoking

Lent is the time for cutting out what's bad.

I'll give up going to bed with men who smoke
for that and other seasons of the year.

Is it the taste? That's not too bad as long
as I don't put my tongue into their mouths.
The tiredness of their skin? Their blood-shot eyes?
Is it the smell of fag-ash in my hair
next day? Not really. That can be washed out,

Post-coital light-up is what worries me.
We've had each other, then the smoking man
turns desperately seeking something else,
scouring the bedside cupboard, pockets, drawers,
he sighs on finding what he really wants,
then's silently unfaithful with his fag.

Some keep their little weapons to themselves.
The worst kind start a sort of troilism.
I don't feel easy with a naked flame
too near my vulnerable naked flesh—
you, me, a cigarette, a smoky kiss—
out of the corner of one eye I see
a toppling inch of ash above a stub
while lover-boy is fiddling with my tits,
foreplay designed to set the bed on fire.

My Prickly Friend

Returning from a party late at night
I went to use the basement loo and saw
a mass of heaving spikes and bright black eyes
and swore I'd never touch champagne again
until I realised that it was real,
a hedgehog struggling in the lavatory pan.

I held a walking-stick—he grabbed the end
and wrapped his body round it like a ball.
(He didn't smell too good when he came out.)
Harry Houdini, Master of Escapes,
I christened him. His black eyes glistened as
I fed him with the leavings from the cat,
then picked him up, a poncho round my hands
to save them from his mass of bristling spines.
I carried him down to the garden's end,
where he could safely graze on juicy slugs.

Next night, at two, my prickly friend was back.
He'd catapult himself into our house
(via the cat-door right above the loo)
then chunder round the basement busily,
night after night. He had no hedgehog friends.
A chortling, snorting presence in my room
would wake me as he scuttled to my side
and tried to tug the blankets on my bed.
I'd stroke his face up from the nose to where
the whiskers turned to bristles on his head.

Four centuries ago, I'd have been burned
for having a 'familiar' friend. These days
it's just peculiar.

Eventually, the novelty wore off.
My hedgehog ceased to come. I like to think
he found a prickly girlfriend on his beat.

One night, before he left, he went upstairs,
wearily climbing steps higher than his height.
I lost him in the house for one whole day.
The following night I caught him, wide awake,
inspecting corners in the room above.

Weeks later, when I'd half begun to think
my nightly visitant had been a dream,
I found the evidence—a prezzie wrapped
in newspaper behind the drawing-room door—
three green-black drolls, tiny as fairies' turds.

Intro Dive (Eilat, 1992)

I'd never snorkelled—hardly stuck my head
beneath the water since I was at school—
but, on an instant's whim, I booked a dive.

A wet suit's shorter from the neck to crutch
than anyone I know, but keeps you warm.
We need a second skin to face the depths.
Unlike the diving girl in Hokusai,
we seek no intimacy with those below—
a passing touch at most. We're there to look.

Beneath the waves, another country lies
with its own set of rules, where humans speak
only in signs and learn to breath again.
(How many times we're all told off as kids
for breathing through the mouth.)
We brave that world, armed with technology.
We have no gills—our air is on our backs
and we must fight our natural buoyancy
with weights strapped round the waist to keep us down.
Our visit's short. It's limited in time.
Goggled voyeurs with large webbed feet,
we walk the ocean floor deliberately
like drunks or astronauts—how fish must laugh.

I keep tight hold of my instructor's hand.
I've held men's hands before but never trusted them.
This time my life depends on one . . .
I get below the surface, then I swim.
The motion's easy, gentle, langorous.
A dolphin swooshes by above my head.
Life's still but fast down there. In, out, in, out—
my bubbled breath streams upward to the air.

My hair flows out and up like tentacles.
Fish pause to look with blasé nonchalance,
then shimmy off—I might be threatening.
The thing that takes to me's a hermit crab.
He slowly makes his way across my palm,
half in, half out of someone else's shell,
his mortgage on his back. I sympathise.

Caught in the fear of trusting someone new,
I've lost all sense of time. The hour is up;
my marriage of convenience must end.
Seeing the bottom all the while, I'm unaware
I've reached the surface. When my face comes out,
I feel bereaved—my water world is lost
and as I walk I feel life's weight return.

Designer Sex
For Demetrios

You've made yourself a master of the art
of touch. You play me like an instrument.
While I lie passively, as you prefer—
eyes closed, you'd rather that I didn't watch—
your fingers (unobserved) combine to seem
like other things. Your subtlety deceives.

This time I'm on my front and sneak a look . . .
I see your hands, then the illusion breaks.
Condoms are not secure enough for you.
You've given up full sex for fear of AIDS.
Your argument is this—why risk disease
when pleasure can be had in different ways?

Of course, I can't pretend I don't enjoy
the mini ecstasies that you create.
You're good at what you do. And yet I feel
a deep frustration every time I come.

Outside upon the street we make a pair—
you in your leather jacket, me in silk—
both tall, we naturally fall into step.
Only within, I feel a certain hollowness.
My womb aches tangibly for something else.

I've journeyed to the limits on my own,
and walked the cities of the world at night.
By Lake Avernus, several years ago,
I drank the waters of the underworld.
This year, I climbed to Mount Lykaion's peaks
where the first Greeks made human sacrifice.
One summit is a mound of ash and bone.
There is a curse, it's said, on men and beasts
who trespass in the Sanctuary of Zeus.

They lose their shadows, die within the year.
(I figure women though, must be immune
my shadow's still as healthy as it was.)
I've slept high up on Mount Taÿgetos,
wedged in between a boulder and a pine,
in summer clothes—the mountain hut was closed.
(You tell me that you walked there as a boy
with several friends—it's near your childhood home.)

In all these places I saw nothing of death.
Avernus now has birds again—and fish.
The stream of Acheron tastes cool and sweet.
Lykaion teems with life—gold butterflies
alighted on my shirt. Taÿgetos
was cold, that's true—but I did not catch cold.
The shepherds gave me hot sheep's milk at dawn.
And as for sex? I've risked it many times
a thing that nobody can do alone.

In all, I find it hard to understand your fear.
Spartans are brave we know from history books—
always in training, athletes, super-fit—
both girls and boys worked out without their clothes.

Sex is the centre and the cause of life.
Foreplay is only foreplay, nothing more.
This holding back—I call it cowardice.
Germs are a part of life—our lottery—
and like fierce dogs, they're most inclined to bite
the timid souls who shrink away from them.
Use some protection till we've found a cure
for AIDS—that's wise—but don't give up on sex.

The end of sex implies a greater death—
all Nature petering out—mankind and beasts
tottering into a fearful old age,
childless—with no hope of posterity.

Choose wisely—caution's best, I'll give you that.
But fearing death too much is fearing life.

Orphic Mystery

The things we listeners take for granted now—
opera, oratorio, recitative,
were all conceived across ten years or so.

A group of men invented opera.
Their aim, they claimed, was a return
to purity—the music of the ancient Greeks.
As all Renaissance Art grew from that source,
now Music, in a slightly later age,
was bound for change.

Dictionaries differ on which opera
was first performed before an audience
These days, now Monteverdi's fashionable,
his *Orfeo* wins the race; but older books
say Peri's *Euridice* came before.
One thing is sure, the story's much the same.
Orpheus the sweetest singer in the world,
whose music charmed the beasts, moved trees and stones,
loses his wife, she's bitten by a snake.
Hades allows him past the gates of hell;
Charon and Cerberus enjoy the songs;
the tortures of the damned are put on hold;
Euridice's allowed to follow him out.
There's one condition though, he must not look
behind for her until they reach the light.
Like Mrs. Lot, Orpheus had to turn back.
What of his later life? He mourns, of course.
But sad songs often are the better ones.

So many versions of his end exist,
it's hard to find the truth about his death.
Some say that Zeus, the father of the Gods,
let loose a thunderbolt and struck him down
for showing mortals sacred mysteries.

Others say the maenads tore him limb from limb;
Dionysos, perhaps, incited this.
Orpheus, while not quite preaching just one god,
revered Apollo more than all the rest.

The poet's head, still singing as it went,
floated right down the Hebros, out to sea,
the Muses gathered up the other bits.
Some parts were swept to Lesbos, Sappho's isle.
A cult was built there round his head and harp,
the better share for any place to get.
The fragments that exist of Sappho's work
show her to be the sweetest of them all
(I don't say greatest, that's another thing.)
Some strain of Orpheus went into her.

We have no ancient music left to us.
The claim of a return to it's far-fetched, and yet,
a few strange parallels exist between
opera's founders and their hero's myth.
The year that Monteverdi finished his work,
his own wife died. Caccini, who composed
some part of Peri's opera and then
went on to do his own, had qualities
that mirrored Orpheus in many ways.
Besides the sweetest singing voice, he could
force nature with his skills—make any plant
bloom at the season of his choice.
Peri, whose long luxuriant golden hair
made him, one might say, an Apollo-clone
sang the god's part in his own opera.
His only son was tutored by the man
who made us see the sun (Apollo once)
as fixed, the centre of the universe.
Whilst Galileo showed no musical bent,

his father was amongst the men whose talk
brought on the birth of opera, although
he died too soon to see its finished form.
Now, Ancient Greece, like Orpheus, is long dead
and Athens chokes with fumes that hide the sun;
its restaurants ring with Zorba's corny hits;
its stones decay beneath the acid rain.

Centuries after Orpheus's bloody end,
a much more subtle death of art ensued:
poetry, solo song went underground
as surely as the River Helicon
anxious (unlike the Hebros) to avoid
complicity in a great poet's death.
Rivers resurface, so do great ideas.
The voice of art, of Orpheus, was reborn.
His singing head washed up on other shores,
became a cult—in Italy this time—
then spread from there across the modern world.

Deus Ex Machina
For Omar

A friend played Cupid in an opera.
Each night, he had to start an aria
while being slowly lowered on to stage—
a Deus ex Machina, complete with wings.
A feather came unglued, one time, floating
remorselessly towards his open mouth . . .
As he inhaled, he took it in and choked.

Eros, brother of Earth, Hell, Darkness, Night,
was born of Chaos in the oldest myths.
In later tales he's Aphrodite's son
and Psyche's lover—still a potent force.
From beautiful young man, he shrank in size
to flying baby pest, equipped with bow.
His form was multiplied and *putti* graced
thousands of walls in ancient Roman homes.
As the religion changed Cupid became
cherubic angels floating in the clouds.
In Italy, he was reborn in poems and songs.
The seventeenth century acknowledged him.
After that brief rebirth he fell again.

Love, once a primal force, is now grown cheap.
We sign the word to several dozen friends.
These days we don't take Cupid seriously.
He's just a logo on some Valentines,
believed in only once a year at most.
We don't appeal to him to set things right
or make a man or woman love us back.

With every person, as in every age,
love is experienced differently.
His first disastrous entry in my life
spread mayhem like my friend's descent on stage.
Eros and all his powerful family

lodged in my mind, spread chaos through my world.
This second time, what shape will he assume?
The son of Venus, or a baby form?

Chess

For Jürgen

I met my first chess-player, New Year's Eve.
The end of a loop outside the circle,
my left arm crossed over my right,
trailed vaguely out, fished for another hand.
You caught me and held on. The clocks struck twelve.
We all sang Auld Lang Syne. We danced until
the party's end. I wanted you right then.

I thought about my childhood games of chess.
My mother'd made a board, plywood with squares
inked black with dye. She bought me a cheap set—
the white men, natural wood that showed the grain.
She thought I'd like to mess around with it,
like Dad's lead soldiers or her button box.
At eight, I taught myself from an old book.
I played at first with men from history,
but thought a real life partner'd be more fun.
My father's female and intuitive brain
could not progress beyond a bout of draughts
so I taught Mum the basics of the game.
Few women learn and few are any good.
Perhaps you need testosterone for chess.
I gave it up at fifteen and a half.

Though I can see the logic of it all
when sitting by the board, just as in life,
after a gambit, I expect to win
and follow through each move with reckless haste.
I find it hard to play a waiting game.

Over the next few days, before you left,
we spent odd hours in bed between your games.
The Congress finished and you went back home.

Our separate lands, our different languages,
stood like the Berlin Wall, held us apart.
That wall's now down, and yet its scar deforms
and, like our pasts, drives wedges in between
those who stretch out their hands across that space
in hope of unity and harmony.

Wolf-Man

For James

Weaned on the Classical—books of Greek gods—
I thought my taste was hairless stone made flesh.
You asked me if I went for hairy chests.
I did the tactful thing and said I liked
most types from hairless up to fairly thick,
but drew the line at fucking chimps or wolves.
'You're in for a surprise,' you said . . .

As surely as the full moon brings a change
to blokes in horror films, the moment that
your suit was off, out sprang the hair.

In ancient times, Arcadians (chosen by lot)
took on the lupine form for nine long years—
traded the human shape for animal—
drew strength from it. I feel that strength in you,
that untamed power. You're hot as fire,
too hot to couch yourself beneath a sheet.
I warm myself against your back and thaw
the ice that years of marble Greek-god-men
planted in shivering shards within my heart.